A Guide For Spiritual Living

I0111411

Also by Kelly R. Jackson

Temporarily Disconnected
A perspective on the decline of Black relationships
and families

Peace In My Mind
The journey to find yourself while embracing who
you are

Scenes From The Blue Book
Poetry, Reflection and the Spoken Mind

And

An Understanding with God
Developing a relationship with God on His terms

A Guide For Spiritual Living

Empowering and uplifting words of wisdom, Vol. I

By

Kelly R. Jackson

A Guide for Spiritual Living
Empowering and uplifting words of wisdom, Vol. I

Copyright © 2011 by Kelly R. Jackson

ISBN: 978-0692333778

Acknowledgements

First and foremost, I'd like to give thanks and all praise to my Lord and Savior Jesus Christ for the inspiration and the strength that He's given to me to complete this work. Lord, You know all of my triumphs and all of my failures, all of my successes and all of my disappointments, all of my supporters and those that oppose me, and yet You've given me the strength to carry on. I couldn't have done any of the things that I've done, especially in the last two years, without you and I am eternally grateful to You for your grace and mercy. Amen!

To my KJWorld Roundtable crew. Thanks for being there as I try to define this work that I'm doing. Thanks for the support, thanks for the love and thanks for being brave enough to discuss any topics that may pop into my head in front of a room full of people and a plate full of chicken tenders. You have my undying gratitude and I truly appreciate you all.

I would like to thank my Aunt Molly and the Mt. Moriah Baptist Church of Omaha, Georgia for allowing me to use a photo of the church on the cover of this book. I consider it an honor and a privilege to be able to share this historic place with all of my readers. It was important to me that on my most spiritual work thus far, that everyone gets to see this holy place where my spiritual foundation comes from. I appreciate you.

As always, I'd like to thank my mother for being the constant inspiration and support for a child that can always use it. You are the truest definition of what a best friend should be. When the battle is fierce, you're always right by my side with words of encouragement, words from The Word or just a hug and a hot meal. I love you always mom.

To my beautiful bride, Ms. Angela Robertson (can't wait to change your last name). I still can't believe that God saved you just for me. Thank you, thank you, thank you for being THE Sunshine in my life. Whenever I wonder if anybody is listening, you remind me that the world is. No matter who's against me, you remind me that if they're against me, they're against us because you're standing right by my side. The measure of our love is that neither of us is happy unless the other one is. If that's not love, then I'm about to come up with another word for it. Thank you for listening, thank you loving and thank you for supporting. Most of all, thank you for pushing me to be what I wanna be and what you see I can be. I don't know how I got this far without you, but I'm glad I won't be going any further without you because you will forever be in my heart. I love you Princess.

KJ

Introduction

When you write a book that threatens to examine your soul, no matter where you are in your spiritual walk, you may be surprised by what you find. That's why this book is a little different from the others that I've written. This book is a partial collection of a weekly email that I send out called "KJ's Weekly Message". As I was putting this book together, I had to go back and gather all of the emails that I thought would work well for this compilation of thoughts. As I printed and printed all of the emails out, it became evident that this would be no ordinary or easy task. I had no idea how many thoughts, how many layers, and how many verses it contained. And when I speak of verses, I'm not speaking of Bible verses. I'm speaking of the verses of my life.

Allow me to give you a little back ground. This all started in February of 2009 as something of a spiritual journal of thoughts. Something that I felt I needed to write for myself and to share with others. I saw things within me, within the church, and within the Christian community that I felt needed to be addressed. While I could see some things in the work that I wanted to get across to others, I was also seeing those things within my own life. Either in the past or in the present, I was using my life to inspire, uplift and bring strength to others. While it was difficult to relive some of those things at times, it also filled me with pride that I was doing something that I encourage others to do all of the time: I was examining myself.

When I decided to do a weekly email back in 2009, I had no idea it would turn into this. I had no idea I'd still be doing that email today. I had no idea it would turn into a book, as my mother suggested it should. I was simply doing what I felt God had put into my spirit to do. Not only has it grown to something that people look forward to on Sunday mornings, I have no idea how many people actually read the email because so may people forward it.

As I've grown in my spirituality over the years, I've found myself going back and searching. I wanted to know how long God had been tugging at me to do this kind of work and how long I had been fighting and ignoring it, without even being conscience of the fact that I was doing so. However, once I begin to allow God to really have His way within my work, things began to change. The email grew. My spirituality grew. My willingness to use my skills for Him grew. I grew.

When you write things of a spiritual nature, you must have a spiritual foundation. My foundation comes from my mother, Annie Jackson-Loritts, and my Pastor and uncle Rev. Dan Flowers. I do what I can to make mention of my mother and my pastor every time I speak of my spirituality because that's where I get it from. They've been my spiritual mentors all of my life and I can't think of better role models in the ways of The Lord. God gave me the gift to write, my mother and my pastor taught me what He would have me to know, and I'm putting all of this together now to carry the message forward.

On the cover of this book is the Mt. Moriah Baptist Church of Omaha, GA. This was my mother's and my uncle's church as they grew from children to adults. This was my grandmother's church and my great grandmother's church. A lot of the Flowers family's spiritual history is within those pews. I felt it fitting to put this church on the front of this book because my mother and my uncle say that's where their spiritual foundation comes from. That means that's where mine comes from.

It actually serves as a metaphor for my work. I've often spoke about how it's at times difficult for me to get people to listen to me because I am my mother's youngest child. There's something about being the baby that leads some people to think that they can't learn anything from you. Even people that are younger than you are struggle with this because even though you're older, if they know you as the baby of anyone's family, they struggle to get past it at times. This is true, even as I am 41 years old. But this little church in the woods of Georgia proves that great things can come from small places.

So if I'm a spiritual descendant of this little church "down home", then what I have to say will have its impact, whether it's the masses that are listening or just a chosen few.

What I want people to understand most about this work, as I do with all of my work, is that these are the thoughts of one man. I don't claim to have all the answers, I don't claim to be right all of the time and by no means am I claiming to be spiritually above anyone. I don't claim to have arrived. I am still and will continue to be a work in progress for as long as I'm here on earth.

I titled this book *A Guide For Spiritual Living* not because I expect it to be your guide, but because it has been my guide. If anyone reading this book adopts it as their guide, it would be a blessing and an honor to me. All I'm trying to do is share my perspective on some things that we face in life and my perspective on the scriptures. I wrote it all in love and I hope that it is received that way.

Also, as it is with all of my work, I hope that you will all be inspired by what I've written here. If I do nothing else but create dialog, then I've done my part. I hope you enjoy and may God continue to shower His infinite blessings on you all. Enjoy.

Kelly

The Opening Message

Week of October 10, 2010

A letter from God...

Dear Children,

I've heard your prayers, your tears and your causes for concern. Believe me, I'm aware of all that you're going through. While I find myself very, very busy these days with the economy, disobedient children, political unrest and people that wanna argue about who I am or whether or not I really exist, I'm never too busy to answer your prayers. But as it says in the roadmap I left you all to follow, everything must be done in divine order.

I do find it interesting that you all seem to want me to respond right away when you call, and yet, at times, you all seem to struggle with following *my* instructions as given. But, I digress. I want you all to know that I'm very aware of what you've been going through. I'm aware of this, I'm aware of that and I'm aware of the things that you wish I wasn't aware of. Let's just say that when you say "Oh my God, I can't believe I did that", I'm thinking the same thing because I know we've talked about it and I know I've taught you better.

I imagine that you often find yourselves wondering why it seems that I don't answer every time you call my name. "Father, Father, Father" is all I hear. And, let me assure you, I do hear you. It's just that there are times when you don't know what you're asking for. There are times when you don't need what you're asking for. There are times I can't believe that you're asking for what you're asking for. And, strangely enough, there are times when I've already answered you. You're just unwilling to accept my answer. But, that's okay. You're still my child and I still love you.

You must know that as long as you believe in me, I'll never stop believing in you. We must maintain that type of relationship if this is going to work. I need you to continue to do my work and I promise to be a constant source of strength for you. I know it gets rough sometimes down there, but you've gotta know that you're never alone. And when you feel that you are, that's when I'm the closest to you. You must remember that when you're at your weakest, that's when I'm the strongest. Lean on me and you'll get through.

I'll need you to make better decisions for yourselves and those around you. I know that things aren't always going the way you want them to. Sometimes it's simply the enemy getting involved, but sometimes it's the decisions that you're making. If anyone knows you're not perfect, it's me. But I need you to try each day to live better.

You must also remember that you not only live for yourselves, but you exist to be a light so that others may find their way to me. I know it's tough when you can't always see the benefits of what I'm telling you to do, but I'm asking you to try it my way and see what happens. I'm asking you to have faith in me. Because I have faith in you.

I want you to try something for me this week. I want you to re-evaluate our relationship. You as the child and me as the parent. Think back on all of the times we've had together as parent and child. Ask yourself, when have I ever let you down? When have I ever left you in despair? When has there even been a moment when you really and truly needed me and I wasn't there? All of those questions should be easy to answer.

Now, let's examine you. How have you been as a child? Have you been obedient? Have you listened when I've spoken? Have you done what I've asked you to? Have you followed the plan that I've set forth for you? Have you kept your end of the deal? If you haven't done these things, you and I aren't on the same page. But, that's okay. I haven't given up on you. We still have time. Just give it some thought for me.

Sincerely,
Your Father

P.S. – Try not to let the only reasons I hear from you be because you're either in trouble or in need. Every now and then, a parent wants a child to call just to say hello.

"Let a man examine himself..."

The Road to Destruction

¹³Enter by the narrow gate. For the gate is wide and the way is easy that leads to destruction, and those who enter by it are many. ¹⁴For the gate is narrow and the way is hard that leads to life, and those who find it are few. – Matthew 7:13-14

We've all heard of keeping up with the Joneses, right? This is one way in which I see this verse. Everybody seems to be trying to do the same things, sometimes to their detriment. We wear what others think we should wear, do what others think we should do, say what others think we should say and all that. Individuality is not the order of the day. Even as we see the consequences of what following the crowd can get you, we continue on as though we're somehow going to come up with a better way.

While these Bible verses tell us how we should seek the Kingdom and eternal life, it is a right now message. It's something we should practice each day of our lives. Often times, we base our actions on what others may think of what we say or do. Not only are we trying to keep up with the Joneses, but now we're trying to impress them as well. We'd rather be wrong and popular than right and unpopular. We'll walk that broad road to destruction, hoping that all who walk with us will embrace us, rather than walk the road to salvation and risk having to walk alone.

While none of us wants to be alone, we all need to accept that it may be a reality of life when you're trying to do right. This is how leaders are born. It's a willingness to follow your convictions, even if no one is following you. I find myself alone quite a bit, not because I'm so much more righteous than others, but mostly because I tend not to share the views of the majority. The way I see it, on the one hand, I don't have an endless phone book full of "friends". But on the other hand, I get a lot of writing done and my phone doesn't blow up with calls from people that aren't genuine, so that's a plus as well. All in all, being willing to stand on my own has made me stronger. And it can do the same for you.

This week, try the narrow gate for a change. Sure, it may be hard, especially if you've never done it before, but just as it is with all the wrong that we're willing to do, you'll get better with practice. Our behavior shouldn't be tailored to what others may say about us or think about us. It should be tailored to doing the right thing. It should be tailored to pleasing God. But be warned. In the process, you may offend some, upset others and some may see you as distant and unsocial. Been there, done that and still there.

Not everyone wants you to do what's right, and most certainly everyone doesn't like to hear what's right. Crazy as it seems, it actually makes some uncomfortable if it's not delivered the way they think it should be. But walking that narrow road isn't about the popularity contests we often find ourselves concerned with. If everyone claims to love you and no one's talking about you behind your back, you shouldn't be pleased. You should be concerned because somebody's faking. But if your eyes are on what's truly important, you'll come to realize that you're never walking alone. He is always with you. And that's all you really need.

You will know them by their fruits

[15]Beware of false prophets, who come to you in sheep's clothing but inwardly are ravenous wolves. [16]You will recognize them by their fruits. Are grapes gathered from thornbushes, or figs from thistles? [17]So, every healthy tree bears good fruit, but the diseased tree bears bad fruit. [18]A healthy tree cannot bear bad fruit, nor can a diseased tree bear good fruit. [19]Every tree that does not bear good fruit is cut down and thrown into the fire. [20]Thus you will recognize them by their fruits – Matthew 7:15-20

Have you ever wondered why you sometimes can't get what you need out of Sunday morning service? While you may show up with the right mind and the right spirit, there may be forces at work that keep you from fully connecting as you should with The Word. Even if you've promised to leave all your troubles at the altar this week, when you get to church, someone else has brought more trouble for you in the spirit of disagreement, dysfunction and negativity. It makes me wonder, if you didn't come to praise Him, then why are you here?

And what about those that we come into contact with in our secular lives? We're always faced with those that claim to have our best interest in mind, but display behavior that doesn't support that notion. While God can send us His blessings through anyone, at any time and on any day of the week, we must remember that the devil has his army, too. Conversely, we can sometimes be spiritually and emotionally self-destructive. We will cut fruit-bearing friendships out of our lives in favor of those that do nothing for us. We will nurture dead relationships in hopes of bringing them back to life. As we harvest spiritually and emotionally, we must become more aware of those trees that are healthy and those that are diseased.

When we hear about false prophets, we automatically assume that it's a church thing. We automatically assume they come in the form of preachers. However, we must remember that we should all be in the vein of prophets. We should all be seeking to spread a harmonious spirit as much as we can. But we must be aware of anyone that comes to us claiming the name of God, but sowing the seeds of discord. We must be aware of ravenous wolves. While it'd be nice to think that we'd be safe from this at church and such people would never darken the doorstep of God's house, we mustn't be deceived. Some of the worst offenders are there. They're in the choir, they're on the usher board, they're bench members and yes, they are sometimes in the pulpit. Remember, the devil comes to church on Sunday morning, too.

Rather than speak to the pastor, these false prophets start cliques and speak about him. Rather than draw souls to Christ, they start their own church services within the services and spread falsehoods. And we become caught up in these things because we are easily distracted when it comes to matters of faith. We're too willing to follow man and not willing enough to follow God. We get so caught up in the singing and the shouting and the "praise and worship", that we forget about The Word of God. We forget about our salvation.

This week, keep your eyes, mind and heart focused on what God would have you do. Whether it's in the sanctuary or in the streets, take no part in the confusion that the devil seeks to bring you. Steer clear of those that bear no fruit, and thus will not see the Kingdom of God. Stay away from those that wish to poison your spirit with their personal agendas. Be wise and acknowledge the spirit in which a person comes to you, instead of accepting the gossip, backstabbing and disrespect for others that they bring. Those of us who haven't studied The Word for ourselves are more susceptible to someone leading us astray. But if you know The Word, you will always know those that are sent by God. You will recognize them by their fruits.

Has a spirit of gossip claimed you?

⁶They visit me as if they were my friends, but all the while they gather gossip, and when they leave, they spread it everywhere – Psalm 41:6

Friends. How many of us have them? Not just a hip hop classic, this is the title of a section in my third book, *Peace In My Mind*. What I covered in that section is what I felt was the deteriorating nature of friendships these days. I talked about the fact that trust seems non-existent these days in friendships. While I spoke on a lot of reasons things are that way, I didn't cover one major reason. Something that destroys more relationships, friendships, families and congregations more than the actual truth can: Gossip.

At the root of all gossip is a spirit of evil. That may seem harsh, but let's take a look at why people really do it. What we're really doing when we gossip is in one way, shape or form, putting someone else down. While some gossip is just us telling what we heard, most times there's a mean spirit behind what we're doing. There's a spirit of deceit as well because we're usually betraying a trust. We're usually gossiping about someone that we know. We're usually talking about someone that has attributed a level of trust to us.

If you trace gossip back to its source, you'll usually find that it's coming from someone close to you. It could be a family member, it could be a spouse or it could be a so-called friend. But make no mistake about it, more times than not, it comes from someone that claims to care deeply for you and swears that they would never do such a thing. I guess that's why they say keep your friends close and your enemies closer. Sometimes, they're one in the same. So now the question goes from "Friends, how many of us have them?" to "Friends, why do we really need them?"

We gossip sometimes because we want to be popular at the expense of anyone's reputation. At times, we simply want to ruin someone's reputation because we don't like them. We're sometimes jealous of someone else's success. We're sometimes reveling in someone's failures. However, just as it is with every other evil thing we find ourselves involved with, we never see this from the other side. We're doing something to someone that we would hate having done to us.

¹⁰Others may accuse you of gossip, and you will never regain your good reputation – Proverbs 25:10

What's amazing to me is how this kind of thing seems to be commonplace amongst people that claim to be Christians and claim to love the Lord. We can't get our souls right, but we're busy being in everyone else's business. More importantly, we can't be about God's business because we're too concerned about who's sleeping with who, who's losing their job, whose marriage is breaking apart and who's on the fast train to hell. Completely unaware that there's a seat reserved for us on that train if we continue this backbiting.

The gossipers usually have a mentality that they either have a right to know everyone's business or a responsibility to spread it. As we talked about in a recent email, we're unwilling to be publishers of peace or to go out and gossip about God, but we have the low down on everyone else's relationship. And we wonder why our love lives are in shambles. And don't get this confused. Just because we have things going on in our lives that we don't want anyone to know about, doesn't mean that it's something shameful. Sometimes, we want to keep things to ourselves for no other reason than the fact that it's our business and no one else's. We have the right to want our business, whether good or bad, to remain our business.

If you're one of those gossipers out there, I want to challenge you. While you're out there spreading rumors, falsehoods or whatever about someone else, try this: For every story, rumor or whatever that you start or continue by telling someone else, try telling one of your secrets at the same time. Tell something they did and then tell something you did that you wanted to keep a secret. Now, I'm no fool. I know that such a thing would never happen. Gossipers are way smarter than that. They don't exist to try and embarrass or degrade or hate on themselves. Only others that they may be envious of.

28 A troublemaker plants seeds of strife; gossip separates the best of friends — Proverbs 16:28

So this week, if you're a gossiper, try turning over a new leaf. I've given you a couple of verses to ponder that represent both sides of the coin. You can be seen as someone that comes as a friend, but then spreads everyone's business all over the place. You can be seen as troublemaker that ruins friendships and brings about discord amongst people. This will in turn ruin your reputation. Or you can find yourself in the verse at the end of this email. One that not only knows the value in having a true friendship, but one that knows the value in being a true friend. It's your choice.

We have to learn to treat each other better. We have to learn to respect each other more. But whether you're the one gossiping or the recipient of the gossip that keeps things going, there are a few things that you must remember. First, that same person that's bending your ear and telling you "dirty secrets" about someone else will soon be talking about you. That's something none of us wants to think about, but it's a reality nonetheless. Second, and most important, we must remember something that's as old as time itself. Life is full of boomerangs. What you put out there will usually come back to you. And what you say about a person behind their backs never remains secret. It always gets back to them. Just something to think about...

13 A gossip goes around telling secrets, but those who are trustworthy can keep a confidence — Proverbs 11:13

Week of May 10, 2009

There is strength in asking for forgiveness

³For I acknowledge my transgressions: and my sin is ever before me —
Psalm 51:3

Do you have it in your heart to ask for forgiveness? We'd all
like to think we do, but not all of us are so brave. We're all
willing to ask God for forgiveness, but how do we do with our
fellow man? We're all good enough to see when someone else
has done us wrong, and twice as good when asking for an
apology. But how many of us have enough strength of
character to not only recognize when we've done someone
wrong, but to go to that person and truly ask for forgiveness? A
few weeks ago, I talked about forgiving others when they've
done us wrong and all I heard from the KJ Congregation was
"Amen!" Now that I'm talking about admitting our own
wrongdoing, I'll be interested to see how quiet my inbox gets.
Sorry. I shouldn't be so hard on Sunday morning.

Forgiving someone is always easier than asking for
forgiveness. When we forgive someone, we're actually in a
position of power. Someone has allowed themselves to be both
humbled and vulnerable, all for the sake of making things right
with us. However, it's how we use that power that defines us.
God is pleased when a person that's done us wrong is willing to
admit that wrongdoing and ask for forgiveness. But we can
turn their sin into our sin by abusing that position of power.
We do that by either being resistant to forgiveness, making the
offending party suffer more than they already have or refusing
to forgive altogether.

Sometimes, we'll seek forgiveness because we're afraid
that tragedy may strike and we may never get the chance to.
Some of us really can be here today and gone tomorrow. But is
that really true forgiveness? Just because we don't get the
chance to say "I'm sorry" to a loved one before they leave here
doesn't change the circumstances of why we were estranged in

~ 13 ~

the first place. Sure, it does diminish the importance of the argument and put things into proper perspective, as no disagreement is more important than the loss of life. But your seeking forgiveness must be pure. It must be because you've done someone wrong and you're really regretful about doing so. While the fact that we don't always have tomorrow can be a motivating factor, your primary reasoning must be because you've wronged your brother or sister.

Often times, we don't want to appear weak, even though we were wrong for whatever it is that we did. Contrary to that thinking, there's actually strength and power in asking for forgiveness. The strong are the ones that are able to humble themselves. The strong are the ones that are able to admit when they've done something wrong and own up to it. But what we have to become better at is recognizing when we've actually done someone wrong. Not only that, but those of us that are offended have to learn to let the offending party know. Not angrily, not furiously and not with a sense of entitlement. We should let them know in a manner that demonstrates how we feel, but doesn't escalate the matter.

Sometimes, people don't know that they've done you wrong. We can't just sit back and assume that we all approve and disapprove of the same behaviors. We get so caught up in what should and shouldn't be offensive by our own standards that we forget to consider someone else's feelings. I've often told my son that it doesn't matter whether or not his actions would've offended him if someone were to do the same thing to him. If what he did offended someone else, whether he agrees with how they feel about it or not, he should apologize. Not necessarily for how you feel, but for offending someone. This is how we all should live.

This week, if you've been holding back your apology, why not let it go? If you've done someone wrong, why not end the bitterness and get it out of your system? One of the difficulties with that elusive forgiveness is the fact that we want to apologize and then have everything go back to normal. Well, I'm not here to lie to you. Sometimes, depending on what we've done, things may never be the same again. And that's okay. We're all human and some wounds can't be healed with a simple "I apologize". Sometimes, it takes time. Sometimes, it never goes away. You can't always get forgiveness on your terms and you can't always give it on your terms. Your peace of mind should come from doing the right thing and being in the will of God. At the end of the day, that's how we will all be judged.

[13]*He that covereth his sins shall not prosper: but whoso confesseth and forsaketh them shall have mercy – Proverbs 28:13*

Week of May 17, 2009

Who are you? A lesson in self-examination, Part 1

¹¹Even a child is known by his doings, whether his work be pure, and whether it be right – Proverbs 20:11

Who are you? If you had to define yourself, what words would you use? And furthermore, how has the way that you've lived your life defined you? These are the questions that have entered my mind over the last week. I strongly believe in self-examination because depending on where others exist in our lives, asking them who we are may not yield the most accurate answers. If someone loves you and cares for you, they may go easy on you. Conversely, if someone doesn't care for you, their comments may reflect that. The only risk with self-examination is the unfortunate fact that we're sometimes more willing to lie to ourselves than others are to lie to us. So if you're ready to be real with yourself, I'll ask you again: Who are you?

Now, this isn't something that I've just decided to ask you. These are questions that I've asked myself as well. While I feel that I've always been a good person, I haven't always lived a good life. If we're being honest here, all of us can identify with that statement. Thus, I've done some things in my past, and maybe even my present, that may cause others to define me as something that I'm not. This is why my work has become so important to me. While I have no interest in keeping up with the Joneses, I've decided to try and live my life in a way that suggests that if the Joneses were to say they can't see God in me, they'd be lying.

Unfortunately, we live in a society where the negative is accented more often than the positive. This means that when others see us, unless they know us well and care for us deeply, our bad deeds will always outweigh the good. While others like to define us by some of the negatives that they see in us, we can't always be mad at that. It's true that we aren't always what we do, but if you're doing whatever that negative behavior is too often, then maybe you are. This can sometimes be tricky because we do make mistakes. We sometimes do things that are outside of our good character, and thus it causes others to think that's who we are all the time.

⁹He that walketh uprightly walketh surely: but he that perverteth his ways shall be known – Proverbs 10:9

We've lost the ability to give one another the benefit of the doubt. Some of us, myself included, are skeptical and cynical to a fault. But some of us are responsible for making people like me the way that we are. Too often, we define ourselves by what we have in a material sense. But the time has long since come for us to start defining ourselves by how we live our lives.

Are you really defined by the money you spend on material things or are you defined by the money you spend doing good for others? Are you the language that you use or is there something more substantial you could be saying to the people? Are you the gossip that you spread or are you more representative of the Word of God that you should be spreading? Are you the jealousy that you feel because another has found love or are you happy to see two people in love that are able to exist in this world filled with hate? Are you solely existing to follow the ways of the world and succumb to all the whims of the flesh or are you willing to exist on a higher plane that puts you on the path to salvation? Who are you?

This week, let your actions be the definition of you. We've talked in these emails about walking on the narrow path, because broad is the road to destruction. If this were something that was easy to do, we'd all be doing it. By definition, it's difficult. The road to salvation is narrow, which makes it hard to always maintain your balance. It's traveled by few, which means that we'll get lonely from time to time. But we must be willing to stay on that path.

Let the work you do here on this earth be what people remember most about you. While we're not always at our best, we can always do our best to be sure that our body of work best represents who we are, as opposed to a blip on the radar or a lapse in judgment being what we're most remembered for. Honest self-examination is the key. It should be as natural as putting on your shoes or brushing your teeth in the morning. Ask yourself each day, who am I? If you don't like what the answer is, don't be discouraged. If you're still alive, you still have time. Just get back on the path.

Who are you? A lesson in self-examination, Part 2

[13]Ye are the salt of the earth: but if the salt have lost his savour, wherewith shall it be salted? It is thenceforth good for nothing, but to be cast out, and to be trodden under foot of men.[14]Ye are the light of the world. A city that is set on an hill cannot be hid. [15]Neither do men light a candle, and put it under a bushel, but on a candlestick; and it giveth light unto all that are in the house. [16]Let your light so shine before men, that they may see your good works, and glorify your Father which is in heaven. – Matthew 5:13-16

I've been told that a lot of you were scratching your heads last week. How dare I ask you to sum up who you are on a Sunday morning? The nerve of that KJ. Doesn't he know where I was last night? Doesn't he know where I woke up this morning? Well, no. I don't know all of these answers, but the best way for any of us to get information is to ask questions. While I'm sure that there are many on the mailing list that knew the answer to that question right away, there were some of you that were taken to a place that you had never been. And that's okay. That's what we do here at KJWorld and that's the purpose of the email. We all have to get in the mirror from time to time for reasons other than vanity. Sometimes, no matter what we do to dress ourselves up, the reflection looking back isn't always pretty.

As we continue on this journey to find out who we are, we must not only look at who we are, but we must look at how we treat others. Sometimes, this is truest representation of who we are. We are very good at trying to get ourselves together in a selfish manner. I'll explain. When we think of self improvement, how many of us think of it in terms of helping someone else to improve themselves? How many of us know how to tithe throughout the week, as opposed to just doing it on Sunday morning? It just got quiet in here.

Part of making ourselves better consists of making this world a better place to live in. I used to tell a friend that was constantly wallowing in self pity that if she couldn't bring herself out of it for her own sake, she should try doing some good for someone else and I promised that it would make her feel better to bring joy into someone else's life. We can find out who we are by looking inward, but we can help to shape who we are by giving outwardly. It can't just be about you. It has to be about us. God has untold blessings for us when we become willing to be used by Him to bless others.

When we finally open our minds to what God has for us, we will see a peace that was unimaginable with a sinful mind. We will know joy that seemed unattainable with an impure spirit. We'll find a love that was so elusive with an impure heart. We'll find a Heaven that seemed impossible to see with a lost soul. We will gain unlimited understanding and lose that sense of confusion that we've had. That confusion had us believing that living right was so hard to do and living wrong was much easier to do. Those of us that have lived wrong realize what a lie this is. In reality, you never realize how much effort sin takes until you give your life to God and He makes everything simple for you. Simply put, He does all the heavy lifting for you.

This week, continue that quest to find out who you are in this world. We have to remember that what we do in this world prepares us for where we'll be in the next world. How we treat one another in this world will determine our fate on judgment day. My intention each week is to share with you the way I think the world should be and how we should all be living in it. I'm trying to make me better by assisting God in making you better. I'm attempting to share with you what I think our roles should be in making this a better place. Not just because I've figured out how to live right. There was never any figuring necessary because I've always had the Word as a guide. I just needed to align myself with it and learn to follow it.

Just like those of you reading my words, I remain a work in progress. Everyday, I'm trying. Some days, I get there.

Other days, I fall short. But that's okay because God is with me on this journey. And while my journey consists of many things, one of them is to deliver this message to you until it becomes a part of my life that's so natural that I'm living it without effort. So where are you in your journey? Working hard or hardly working?

October 26, 2010

The journey and the destination

Are you on your way or are you already there? As I've grown closer to God, I've noticed that we ultimately have two sets of Christians. The Journey Christians and The Destination Christians. Here's the way I see them:

Destination Christians

These are the Christians that are more focused on the destination than the journey. While there's nothing wrong with being focused on their destinations, at times they're so focused on Heaven that they forget to do the things they need to do on earth. At times, they've already placed themselves in Heaven, sometimes seated at the feet of Jesus. Because they're already home, they see no need to go out and show others how to get there.

These Christians are so enlightened that they're able to tell you when you've fallen short, whether you've really changed like you say you have, whether you've forgiven as you say you have and even whether or not you're doing enough to get into Heaven as they have. These Christians have the ability to look inside your heart and tell you whether or not you're saved. None of these acts are ever based on the Word. They're always based on their "gift". God is not pleased with the Destination Christians. Simply because they have no Heaven or hell to put anyone in. And if they don't learn to focus more on their own salvation, they will arrive at a destination that they hadn't anticipated.

Journey Christians

These are the Christians that are aware of the journey they're on. They're aware that their journey leads to their destination. They're aware that they do fall short. They've acknowledge to themselves and to God that they will have to try each day to live right. They understand that they're a work in progress. They understand that they can learn about how God wants them to live by studying His Word, not just by listening to their own thoughts and doing things from their own perspective.

They understand that they've yet to arrive, so there's still work to do. They understand that being led by the Holy Spirit is the way to salvation. They understand that the Holy Spirit would never lead them to judge anyone because the Word speaks against it. They understand that the Holy Spirit would never lead them to condemn anyone because that's what the Word is for. God is pleased with the Journey Christians. He can use them to do His work as they continue on their journey. He can use them to spread His Word. He's pleased because He knows He has something to work with.

A lesson in commitment

³Trust in the LORD, and do good; so shalt thou dwell in the land, and verily thou shalt be fed ⁴Delight thyself also in the LORD: and He shall give thee the desires of thine heart ⁵Commit thy way unto the LORD; trust also in Him… – Psalm 37:3-5

Commitment can be a funny thing. While the word itself suggests something solid, it can be something very, very loose. In fact, we can change the meaning completely depending on what we're claiming to be committed to. Most times, the level of a commitment depends on the person giving it. That usually determines how much it's worth and how strong it will be. But I've noticed something. Many of us expect a level of commitment that we're unwilling to give in return. At the same time, we foolishly commit ourselves to things that promise diminishing returns.

Let's examine this for a minute. Are you willing to give 100%, even if you're not getting the same thing in return? On the surface, most of you said no, but I'll prove my point shortly. Another question, how many of you can work a job to the best of your ability everyday, even if you don't like that job, but simply because you value your reputation as a professional, your good name as a hard worker is at stake and you're simply grateful to God that you have a job? Have you confused commitment to yourself and your own reputation with your commitment to the job? Have you figured out that hard workers are hard workers and you can't pay someone to give you an effort that they really don't wanna give you? We humans are quite creative. If we're not willing to give you our all, make no mistake about it, no matter what you pay us, we'll figure out how not to give you what you're paying for in return.

Better yet, how many of us have dress codes that we adhere to on our jobs? If you ignore the dress code, you could be fired. So we abide by the rules in the name of survival. There's money involved, so we do what we're told. But what about church? We have a new way of dressing when we come to church. In the name of saving souls, we've adopted a come as you are mentality, even though the pay on this job is much greater. But why does it seem that some of us are simply trying to take advantage of God? Are we no longer willing to "dress to impress" when it comes to God?

We've taken come as you are to the next level and we don't even give God a good effort on Sunday morning. But if the nightclubs tell us to dress to impress because it's ladies night and drinks are free until 11pm, we not only step our wardrobe game up, we'll go out and buy a new outfit for the occasion. How many of us have gone out and bought a new outfit just to go to church in when Easter wasn't involved? While I believe that God will allow you into Heaven based on how you lived as opposed to how you dressed for church, why do we take advantage of His willingness to give us free will?

How many among you have given your all to a relationship that was doomed to fail no matter what you did? The more love you give out, the less they give back. The more committed you wanna be, the more they wanna be free. The more you try to hold on, the more they let go, only to try and come back when you finally give up and let go for good. Been there, done that. Why can't we give God that love instead? This is the one relationship that you can have in your life with a guaranteed success rate. If it ever doesn't work out, it's not Him, it's you.

How long is that lottery line this week? Rather than put our faith in God, we'd rather try and quick fix our problems with a few million dollars, never counting up all of the dollars we waste on losing tickets. Never realizing the fact that if we're not in the will of God, no matter how many millions we amass, it will all go away. We've committed ourselves to the cigarette and alcohol companies of the world, giving them all that we earn weekly in an effort to kill ourselves slowly, while their businesses get healthier and healthier. Question: Since our economy has crumbled, how many stories have you heard of companies that sell products that are a detriment to our health struggling financially? Think about that.

This week, recommit yourself to God. This is the only way to success on the job, success with your finances, success in your health and success in your love life. It doesn't make sense that we're more willing to follow the rules of society than the rules of the Bible. We're sometimes so backwards in our lives. Everyday, we question sure things in our lives, while things that need attention and correction slip through the cracks and get worse and worse.

It doesn't make sense that we refuse to give God 100% commitment and yet we expect that from Him. We have to learn to put our best foot forward for God. We have to learn to give Him our best because not only are we always asking Him for His best, He's always giving it. And contrary to popular belief, we don't always deserve it. Maybe it's time to stop "praying" for that 3 or 4 digit to fall and place a bet on God. You will never lose that one.

Are you properly using the blessings you've already been given?

[12]Blessed is the nation whose God is the LORD; and the people whom He hath chosen for His own inheritance – Psalm 33-12

If there is one common theme that seems to exist with a lot of Christians it is the idea that we deserve blessings. We feel as though we should live a blessed life even when we haven't done all that we should to earn what we're asking for. While some of us do deserve the blessings we receive, most of us are asking for things that we don't deserve. So the questions remain: How hard have you really worked for God? When was the last time you told someone how good God was without using something of a material nature as proof? Are you leading someone to Christ simply by living right or are you leading them astray? And instead of checking God for your missing blessing, how willing are you to check yourself?

There are certain rules that apply to being blessed. There is work that we must do for God. We sometimes fail to realize the role that we have in soul saving. It's not all on the preacher, it's not all on the deacon, it's not all on the missionaries in church, but it's on all of us to lead souls to Christ. We not only have to try and be on our best behavior, we also have to be an example for others. This is extremely important to those of us that are adults. Because we have so many young people looking to us as examples, we have to give them something of substance to look to. One of the worst things we can do is lead a child astray. Young minds are looking to us to mold them, and yet we're willing to lead them into self destructive behavior.

Make no mistake about it, our young people don't become stupid on their own. Our young people can't become lost without an adult to help them. I'm seeing this one firsthand in my life right now. One of the reasons I stayed on track as a youth was because I had no safe haven to run to. There were no adults for me to go to that wouldn't try to uphold what my mom taught me. Even if they were a shoulder to lean on from time to time, their message was always the same: Honor thy father and thy mother. If you aren't delivering this message to the youth of today, not only will you miss out on your blessings, you will be punished. These are not just your children or my children, these are God's children.

Financially, things look bleak for us as a nation right now. As I look around the city that I live in and see the fallout from major automobile makers filing for bankruptcy, it saddens me to see so many losing their jobs. While it's hard for anyone to feel blessed at a time like this, I can't help but wonder, have we tied our own hands?

I'm not sure where we thought we'd end up in this city and in this country when we decided we didn't need God. We stopped praying in schools and though it'd be okay. We stopped going to church and thought we'd be okay. So many of us in this city jumped on TV and radio, gathered at homes, barbeques and barber shops and talked extensively about how the Mayor of Detroit should lose his job. Then we all shouted with glee when it happened. But now that the cement shoes are on the other foot, I wonder how we feel now? When people suggested that we pray for that man and this city, so many scoffed at the idea. But how many misplaced workers are clamoring for those prayers right now?

We've discussed this before in these emails and it seems appropriate to do it again. There's nothing too hard for God and He has many blessings for us to receive. But all of these blessings are not tithe related. We can't treat church like the casino where we put a certain amount of money in and expect to get more money out. You can go to church four Sundays a month and five when we have them. You can shout hallelujah all you want when you get there. You can leave all the tithes in the storehouse and then some if you like. But if you aren't fully engaged in your walk with God, if you're not about your

Father's business every day, if you're planting seeds of disharmony, discord and confusion in someone else's life, you will miss out of crucial blessings.

This week, make it right with God. But this time, do it for all the right reasons. So often, we go to our knees when we want God to do something for us. I'm sure there are a lot of people in the city of Detroit doing just that these days. But we as a people have to learn to give back to God simply because we owe Him so much. If you lost a job this week, you will still be blessed if you stay within His will. If you haven't been the best example of living right to those around you, there's still time to do that. As our verse suggests, if we recognize God as our Lord, we shall receive His inheritance. The best thing about the God we serve is the fact that no matter how much we give up on Him when He doesn't do what we ask Him to do, He never gives up on us for exhibiting that same behavior.

Week of June 14, 2009

Taking responsibility for your life

[7]Be not deceived; God is not mocked: for whatsoever a man soweth, that shall he also reap. [8]For he that soweth to his flesh shall of the flesh reap corruption; but he that soweth to the Spirit shall of the Spirit reap life everlasting – Galatians 6:7-8

Have you taken control of your life or is it still in someone else's care? When things aren't as they should be in your life, how much responsibility do you assess to yourself? When something goes wrong in our lives, we immediately look to place the blame on someone or something else. We have a long list of people and circumstances that are to blame. However, when you go down that list, our names are either at the bottom of the list or not there at all. So how much responsibility do we have for what happens in our lives and how much can we really do about it?

We sometimes suffer from misfortunes in our lives and pretend we don't know how any of it happened. But what we must accept as a people is the fact that sometimes we're our own worst enemy. There are a lot of things wrong in our lives that are completely our fault. We go out and mistreat people on a daily basis, and yet we wonder why we aren't blessed. We put our own personal misery out into the world, never expecting it to come back to us. But our actions are like boomerangs. Whatever you put out into the world will come back to you. If you use, you will be used. If you abuse, you will be abused. If you lie, cheat and steal, be ready for that to come back to you. It really makes you wonder, with all the things that happen to us in our lives just being Christians, why would we go out and invite more misery by being miserable people?

This behavior is detrimental to our mental and spiritual well being, but we can't shake it because we refuse to acknowledge when we doing wrong. We continue to suffer from self inflicted wounds with no healing in sight. We stay in spiritual, emotional, physical and financial ruts when a simple change of our ways and behaviors could free us from all that's ailing us. When our relationships fail, we blame others while never examining ourselves. We blame our partners, even though we enabled them in all of their "wrong" behavior. We blame outsiders for getting into our business, even though we told them all of our secrets. When our money runs short, we blame the job that God blessed us with for not paying us enough, but we never blame ourselves for not wisely managing what we do receive.

However, my favorite excuse is Lucifer. I could imagine that the devil himself wonders on occasion how his name is always coming up when someone needs to be blamed for something. We Christians lean heavily on this crutch. I'm well aware of the devil's presence in our daily lives. If for no other reason, it's evident in some of the behavior of us "Christians". I'm well aware that he shows up uninvited and wreaks havoc from time to time. But again, I ask, where is your responsibility? There are ways to get the devil out of your life, but you have to want him gone. The reality of the matter is, sometimes the devil shows up because he *was* invited. Sometimes the devil won't leave because we won't let him go.

This week, it's time to own up to it. If the troubles in your life can be attributed to your behavior, then you must own that. It's the only way you can make it right. As this week's verse suggests, if you do good things, good things will follow you. But if you don't, you have no one to blame but yourself when good things don't happen in your life.

One of the most dangerous habits a person can develop is always blaming someone or something else for everything that goes wrong in their lives. You have to assume responsibility for your own life. You can't blame it all on the devil when it goes wrong and you can't put it all on God to make it right when you screw up. And trying to fix a week's worth of misbehavior, misdeeds and mistreatment of your fellow man can't be handled in 3 hours of church on Sunday morning. If it took you a week to tear it up, then it may take just as long to fix it.

As I said, we have enough going wrong in our lives without doing things to ourselves. We have to resist the desire to befriend the devil. And while he is a presence, we can't put it all on him. Most of us do wrong with little to no provocation. Satan isn't holding a gun to anyone's head. But if you let him ride with you, soon enough, he'll be driving. And as it was for those of us that were raised by good parents, you can follow your friends if you want to, but you're responsible for your own behavior.

The pyramid scheme

⁹Keep therefore the words of this covenant, and do them that ye may prosper in all that ye do –
Deuteronomy 29:9

I'm working on something new this week. Follow me, if you will. It's the KJWorld Pyramid Scheme. All I need you to do is tell 3 people about this email, and then get them to tell 3 more people about this email, and so on and so on. Can I get you all on board? While some of you said yes, some of you asked, "What's in it for me?" If you asked that last question, not only is it a fair and legitimate question, it's a necessary question. One that we often ask when approached by someone to join one of these pyramids. While the question is legit, what we require as an answer in order to join is a bit suspect.

If you're unaware or don't watch the news, people are being brought down weekly for pyramid schemes. What's interesting to me is how many people were unaware that all of their money was being stolen from them until our economy went down the tubes. They blindly put their trust in someone that simply sold them a dream. All they were offered in return was what would make them happy: more money. These people never thought to check any of this out until they thought that their million dollar homes and lifestyles were in jeopardy. Once they were reminded or found out the hard way that only the people at the top of the pyramid really get rich in these things, they were devastated. While I would never wish such misery on anyone, it seems a bit shortsighted to just blindly trust anything earthly.

If my proposition at the beginning of this email was real and I told all that were reading this that there was money in it, my inbox would blow up. Because the promise of money is something that man is always willing to pursue, even without seeing any real evidence of attaining it. In the midst of financial turmoil, buckling down and working harder is no longer an option. Getting rich quickly moves to the forefront.

We are a microwave society. We slowly work ourselves into a problem and then try to remove ourselves quickly. Never realizing that all we're doing is sinking deeper and deeper into despair. That's why things like pyramids are so popular. In fact, I may even ask you to bring me money in order to get you rich. It takes money to make money, ya'll. But I have a few questions: Why are we more willing to sign up a friend for money than we are to sign one up for Heaven? What does it take for us to be spiritually rich? And what kind of investment does it take for us to be successful in God's pyramid?

While money seems to be at the center of all that we do these days, if you're a Christian, you must maintain your perspective in this life in order to be in position for the next life. It's amazing what we're willing to put our faith in if someone says we'll get rich. At the same time, we refuse to follow God with that same kind of faith because we can't always see all of the blessings that He's promised us. Although we've all seen what He can and will do in all facets of our lives, we still refuse to follow. I mean, seriously. All He's offering is everlasting life. The guy at the seminar told me I could be a millionaire in a year if I just sign people up and sell like my life depended on it. It seems so easy and Christianity is so hard. Or so it would seem until all your money dries up.

This week, let's try to sign up 3 people in God's pyramid. Once you do that, see if they can sign up 3 more people. And so on and so on. But here's the "drawback": you may not get your reward here on earth. It may not be that new car, a new house or even a million dollars. Your reward may be waiting in Heaven. In fact, your reward may be the fact that you get to see Heaven. Your reward may be the Kingdom of God. How does that grab you? The only investment that you need is faith. Faith that God will do exactly what He said in His Word.

I'm sure there may be some reading this that will question what I've written here. Some may tell me that God wants us to be financial "prosperous" while we're here on earth. However, I submit to you that God simply wants us to be prosperous. While that could be financial, it could also mean in the way of knowledge. You could also prosper in the way of having good and obedient children. You could also prosper in the way of community and the impact that you have on yours. Or, like me, you could prosper in your work.

Just by the fact that some of you have signed up for this email and continue to encourage me in what I do, I feel as if I'm prosperous. I feel that I am blessed. I feel that I'm doing the will of God. And as long as I do that, I will be rewarded. God will see to it that my work reaches all the people that He wants it to reach and touches all of those that it's meant to touch. No monetary promises necessary, only spiritual. No need to sign up under me in order to get your "riches". I'll put you in touch with the head of the pyramid and you're sure to be blessed.

Dying so you can live

[3]Jesus answered and said unto him, "Verily, verily I say unto thee, except a man be born again, he cannot see the Kingdom of God" – John 3:3

Have you had your death today? That is an interesting question, don't you agree? How can you die and yet still be alive? We have love songs that talk all the time about dying inside. And yet, you're singing this song to me. Interesting. We often claim that we're "starving to death", when most of us have no idea about such things. In fact, as a nation, we're obese. Hmmm. We've even over dramatized our jobs and claimed that we're being worked to death. And yet, we party every pay day. Maybe it's not as dire as we make it sometimes. That's evidence that we can be so casual about death that we'll insert it into anything. But how many of us are really ready to die? And if you died today, what kind of legacy have you left? Lastly, can you die today and not be concerned about your soul?

If we intend to leave a legacy that we can be proud of, we must become more concerned with the state of our souls. We must walk with God while we're here on earth. The Bible asks us in the 3rd Chapter of Amos, "Can two walk together except they be agreed?" In order for us to walk with God, we're gonna have to be in agreement with Him. And in order to accomplish that, we're all gonna have to die a little bit.

There are things about you that can't continue to exist if you really intend on seeing the Kingdom. We were put here to be Christ-like in our ways. And while we can't *be* Christ, we can be like Him. And like Christ, we all need to be willing to have a death in order to have a resurrection. It's up to you to figure out what that is for you and make the necessary adjustments. And just as it was when Jesus died, there is joy in the resurrection. But in order to truly be born again, you must first be willing to die.

If we become more mindful of where we'll spend the afterlife, it can affect the way we live in this life. Our souls must become more of a priority than the things that we focus on so often. Materialism must die in the black community and in the Christian community. A better sense of community must be resurrected in its place.

The recklessness that our children have must die. The bus stops aren't even safe for them anymore as they travel to and from school. The lack of respect that they have for their bodies, for one another, for their parents and for human life in general, must die. Better role models, one's that don't curse at them through rhymes or encourage "birthday sex" in every line of their so-called music, must be resurrected instead. This is where the church used to step in and save the day, but unfortunately we're not playing our position anymore. Because we have lost our identity in the church, we have also lost our identity in the black community.

I'm not sure about you, but I'm at a point where I wanna get better each day. I wanna change a negative to a positive every day. I feel that I can change the world and you should feel the same way too. But in order to change the entire world, I must change my individual world first. This has to be an ongoing process to see God face to face. We can't be "kinda saved". There are no part-time jobs in spirituality. You can't be satisfied being somewhere in the middle. There is no middle ground with God. You're either with Him or you're not.

At this stage in my life, I'm trying not to waste a lot of time. Some of my early years were wasted on unproductive living. At certain points, I either missed my calling to do more work for God or I heard the call and just didn't answer. Through my writing, I've been given another opportunity to change lives. What I write will be here long after I'm gone. And that's how I'm creating my legacy. Ain't God good?

This week, be the Christian that's willing to die a little. Die so that you can be resurrected. Here's your challenge: Find three things about yourself that you need to change and make it happen. If you're being honest, this won't be hard at all. All of us have lists that far exceed the three things that I'm calling for. But we have to start somewhere. Old ways have to die. Old habits have to die. Old language has to die. In fact, some of the new language has to die even before it gets old. There are so many things that have to go away in order to experience a brand new you. These things have to go away in order experience a brand new life. And our God is so merciful, that He's willing to give you time. But don't wait too long. Tomorrow isn't promised, but today is already here. Now is the time. Have you had your resurrection?

Week of July 19, 2009

Making a deal with God

[21] Then Jesus beholding him loved him, and said unto him, "One thing thou lackest: go thy way, sell whatsoever thou hast, and give it to the poor, and thou shalt have treasure in Heaven: and come, take up the cross, and follow me - Mark 10:21

In life, we often find ourselves in one of three positions: The position to compromise, the position to sacrifice or the position to trade. Of course, knowing this is only half the battle. Knowing when to do which is the true test. While it's good to have the ability to compromise, there are certain areas in our lives in which we do so to our detriment. In these instances, I contend that we're not compromising, but rather trading. As discussed at the KJWorld Roundtable, in my eyes, these two things seem to be the same, but in fact, they're very different.

Sacrifice and compromise are more similar to me because more times than not, they're being done for the greater good. But trading is completely different. When you're trading, it's not always about the greater good. You trade to gain an advantage on someone, even if it isn't the person you're trading with. It's not always this way, but it is for the most part. I know this all seems like semantics, but follow me. Have you ever given up something of value and gotten little to nothing in return, all the while convincing yourself that a compromise was taking place when there was simply a trade being made? Long question, I know, but ask it anyway.

For example, I can go to the store and give a man behind the counter almost $10 and he'll give me something that could give me and all those around me cancer. Outstanding. Not really a fair trade in retrospect, but one that many of us are all too willing to make on a daily and sometimes twice daily basis. Or, how 'bout this. At 2 or 3am, I can go to White Castles and give someone at the drive-thru window a few dollars and he'll give me something that will have my stomach doing cartwheels for the next 24 hours. A great time will be had by all in the bathroom, I'm sure. Or you could go out and marry someone that's notoriously promiscuous and they can do you the favor of continuously cheating on you, having outside children or, God forbid, giving you a disease. Anyone excited about the possibilities yet?

Too often, we over simplify things in our lives. We make it too convenient. However, some things go beyond the surface. We have to be willing to dig deeper. This phrase is heard often at the Roundtable: "Think it through". Compromise isn't simply giving up one thing for another. It's more about coming to an agreement that all involved can benefit from. Some would say that they compromise to keep the peace, but that doesn't always work either. In fact, compromise may come about without any immediate peace being achieved. So when we find ourselves in unproductive relationships, friendships, jobs, spiritual relationships or whatever, are we "compromising" in an effort to get what we need in order to be happy or are we simply trading true happiness for temporary satisfaction?

These are questions that we need to ask ourselves spiritually as well. That verse at the top of the page is powerful, isn't it? How much are we willing to sacrifice for God? In that situation, we would be like the young, rich ruler in that verse. We would walk away sorrowful if Jesus told us to sacrifice all we had and follow Him. We seem to be willing to trade our place in Heaven for the pleasures of this earth. And while following God is about sacrifice, you shouldn't sacrifice Heaven for earthly things. It should be the other way around. We'll give up our morals, values and beliefs to stay in fruitless relationships and friendships, but what will we give up for a God that can give you everything you desire and more?

We even find ourselves looking to compromise with God. How ridiculous is that? Can you really go to the negotiating table with God? What do you have to offer? I'll come to church if you bless me. I'll do right by my wife if you bless me. I'll be a better wife to my husband if you bless me. If you promise me more money, I'll tithe. But how is that compromise? What does God really get out of our obedience? While it pleases Him, there's no gain for anyone but us. He already owns everything. The earth and the fullness thereof. God simply wants to trade with you. In fact, this isn't a fair trade and God is losing because even though we don't always deserve it, He blesses us anyway. But that's just how great He is.

[39]He that findeth his life shall lose it; and he that loseth his life for my sake shall find it – Matthew 10:39

This week, let's work on the deal that we *should* be making with God. Give God your life for the greater good. Do this one thing and watch some of those unproductive situations that I spoke of get better or disappear all together. It will amaze you. Start off with sacrifice. Sacrifice your time, your body, and yes, even your money in service to God. And then, make the trade. We give Him our lives and He gives us *eternal* life. We're winning all day on this one, but He's still willing to do the deal. So you best be taking it before He pulls it off the table.

And while we all like to think we're getting over, He knows He's giving more than you're giving and He's okay with that. He loves you that much. Don't believe what I'm saying is true? Don't rush into it. Take your time. Do your research. Ask someone who's made the deal how things are going for them. Just know that life is short and this is a limited time offer. So go ahead. Think it through.

Promoting the business of God

¹Bless The Lord, O my soul: and all that is within me, bless His holy name ²Bless The Lord, O my soul and forget not all His benefits ³Who forgiveth all thine iniquities; who healeth all thy diseases ⁴Who redeemeth thy life from destruction; who crowneth thee with loving kindness and tendermercies – Psalm 103:1-4

Have you ever had a bad service in your life? For example, if you went to a restaurant or hotel and the service was horrible, would you go there again? Probably not, I'm sure. But not only would you not go there again, if someone asked you to suggest a good hotel or restaurant, not only would you suggest somewhere else, you may even go out of your way to warn them not to go to those places.

Sometimes, unprovoked, you'd explain in great detail the service you got. We'd do this for people that we cared greatly for or for casual acquaintances. Word of mouth is powerful in the business world. Some of you are reading this email because you either heard about it from someone else or had it forwarded to you. So, why can't we do for our own lives and past experiences what we'd do for some place that didn't give us enough hotel towels like we asked for?

For some of us, talking about past life experiences can be scary. In most cases, we're talking about the foolishness of youth and all of the mistakes that come with it. In other cases, we're talking about being a little bit older and not quite focused on where we should be in our lives. And all of the mistakes that come with that. All of us take different roads in life to become the people that we are. Because we're human, we make mistakes along the way. Some of them small and ultimately insignificant, and others a little more major with different consequences. But when we do make mistakes, we all seem to wanna bury them as soon as we can. We want to leave no evidence of our misbehavior, evil deeds, lapses in judgment or just plain ol' stupidity. We're so busy trying to bury our pasts that we forget how important it is to who we are today. But all in all, is having a past really all that bad?

It's true, some things are important to leave in the past. In the past, some of us were involved in unproductive friendships, unproductive relationships and we had unproductive ways. But, it's been said that those who don't learn from history are doomed to repeat it. So while we may wanna bury those missteps and misdeeds, it may be in our best interest not to forget them. The way I see it, your past, whether good or bad, should be your testimony. Just as it is in the example that I used, we're willing to testify to others about where we've been to eat or sleep, and if it wasn't a good experience, we warn others so that they don't experience it as we did. If you're a better person today, your past could be something that shows others how far you've come.

Too often, especially in the Christian community, we try to ignore the things that we did in the past and show people the picture that we want them to see. But I'm a witness to the fact that it's my past that determined who I am today. It's my past that makes me write these words to you on each Sunday morning. It's my past that set me up for a brighter future. If I never had an example of how wrong I was, I'd have no idea of how right God can make me if I just stay on the path that He's set for me.

What we must remember is that we can use our life experiences to shape someone else's life in a positive way. We can't walk through life with our newfound connection with God and pretend that we never had one with the devil. This is especially important with our youth. Our children won't always listen, but we must share our experiences with them anyway. When our young people get off track, we can't just get on them, telling them what thus said the Lord, as if we don't recognize their behavior. We were once foolish young men and women, too. It's important that they know why we think they're wrong. Not because we're so holy, but because more times than not, we've been where they are.

This week, don't hide from your past. In fact, you can talk about it loudly. If you were somewhere dark in your life, but now you see the light, this is the perfect opportunity to tell someone how good God is to you. This is the perfect opportunity to talk about how God brought you out. Too often, we only wanna speak loudly about how God brought us out of sickness or poverty. How about talking about how God brought you out of promiscuity. How about talking about how God brought you out of gambling. How about talking about how He brought you out of drinking and drugs. How about speaking on how He delivered you from adultery. Maybe talk about how He stopped you from lying and backstabbing. Testify about that in church for a change. But only if you've stopped these things, mind you.

All of these people with all of these afflictions either come to church or come into contact with us daily. Let them know that while we're letting our light shine for Christ now, we weren't always so pure. In fact, we all still fall short. Allow them to see some of themselves in you while you're representing something new. Let them know that no matter where they are or where they've been, God is in the business of saving souls. Tell them about the great service God has given you. Because, as we all know, word of mouth is good for business.

Week of August 23, 2009

Maintaining your focus on God

[28]And Peter answered Him and said, "Lord, if it be thou, bid me come unto thee on the water"[29]And He said "Come". And when Peter was come down out of the ship, he walked on the water to go to Jesus. [30]But when he saw the wind boisterous, he was afraid; and beginning to sink, he cried, "Lord, save me". [31]And immediately Jesus stretched forth His hand, and caught him, and said unto him, "O, thou of little faith, wherefore didst thou doubt?" – Matthew 14:28-31

Here in the City of Detroit, we've watched as corruption was revealed in our city's government. It was something that initially divided our city. The media had many believing that all the corruption existed in one man, our former mayor. I warned all who would listen to my spoken words and through my website not to place all of the blame on this one man. The kind of corruption we were seeing always runs deeper than one person.

As we watched city council members posturing on television, most posing as bus drivers ready to throw the mayor right under, I couldn't understand how they couldn't see that once he was removed from office, this same media would have no choice but to focus their attention on them and all of their wrongdoing. This is how the media works. This is how life works. This is how the devil works. He has desired to have you that he may sift you as wheat.

Often, these types of things happen in our own lives, just as they happened in the mayor's life and in the lives of those council members. We receive a certain measure of success in life and we automatically assume that we did all of this by ourselves. We assume that our talent, our brilliance and all of the things that make us so wonderful are the reasons for our successes. While we often say "Thank you Jesus" when something positive happens, it seems to be something we say in the same vein as another one of life's catchphrases. We don't say it with a true appreciation for what God has done for us. As this city's leaders have done, we take our eyes off of Christ and, subsequently, we begin to sink into troubled waters.

Something we speak about often in these emails is, for lack of a better term, when we should give God some attention. It's often heard in spiritual circles that we should call on God in times of trouble. While that's always sound advice, we should remember to call on God sometimes just to say "Thank you". Thank Him for what He's done for you, thank Him for what He's doing for you and thank Him for what He's going to do. But sometimes, as hard as we may try, we're not always able to avoid the troubled waters of life. Our best laid plans to smoothly sail through life may go astray at times. But as this week's verse proves, there's a way to navigate those rough waters.

We have to understand that when we become successful in Christ, the enemy's attacks become more severe. The waters get rougher. We're more aware of man than we are of the devil. We're more aware of the "haters" than we are of who sent them to hate on us. I've seen this on my job as I'm sure you've seen it on yours. I've seen this in relationships and friendships as I'm sure you have. I've seen this in my community as I'm sure you've seen it in yours. I've even seen it in this work that I feel that I'm doing for God as I'm sure you've seen it in any works that you've done for God. When you shine for The Lord, people notice. And if they're working for the enemy, they're not pleased.

As it is in this week's verse, we must learn to keep our focus. We have to learn to follow God's commands. When we hear His voice leading us to a place, we must go to that place. At the same time, when He's leading us *away* from a place, we must learn to go as commanded. Sometimes, we're in rough waters because we won't move on from a place that God has deemed no longer a good place for us. Wrong jobs, wrong man, wrong woman, wrong places to hang out and even wrong churches. If God says to let it go, we must let it go. Otherwise, we begin to sink as Peter did. We not only take our eyes off of Jesus, but we lose faith in what He's already told us we can do. It's not blasphemous for me to think that I can walk on water just as Jesus did. Peter was a flesh and blood man, just as I am. All he had to do was keep his eyes on Christ and he would've never begun to sink. This is what we must do everyday.

This week, don't let it be about you all the time. While you are talented, while you are strong, while you are gifted, remember that it was God that blessed you with all of the tools to be successful. Often in the black community, we implore those that become successful to not forget where they've come from. This should be true in the Christian community as well. If you pray when you're poor, pray when you're rich. If you pray during tough times, pray when everything's alright. But most importantly, remember that we're all human. Just as Peter did, we all take our eyes off Christ from time to time. However, my favorite part of that verse is when Peter began to sink. Jesus was right there to catch him. Even when our faith is lacking, we can still be saved. He will never let you drown.

Week of August 30, 2009

Fiction vs. Reality: The line between what we claim to be and what we really are

²²The light of the body is the eye: if therefore thine eye be single, thy whole body shall be full of light ²³But if thine eye be evil, thy whole body shall be full of darkness. If therefore the light that is in thee be darkness, how great is that darkness! ²⁴No man can serve two masters: for either he will hate the one, and love the other; or else he will hold to the one and despise the other... - Matthew 6:22-24

I recent asked a question on Facebook about how real people are when they get on the internet. If you ever wanted to see another side of a person, catch them on the internet. We treat it as if what we say or do there doesn't count. We act as though we can dismiss our behavior as a Hollywood actor would dismiss a less that desirable character that he may have played in a movie. It's not real and it has no effect on my life or who I am. And while there is an element of fantasy to the internet, these things that come out do exist deep inside us somewhere. As I also asked on the internet, do we realize that an alternate universe, though not real, can in fact affect your reality?

What's interesting to me is the fact that our behavior seems to be modified based on where we are or who's watching. This is where our ability to be internet characters comes from. A lot of times, we're dealing with people on the internet that we don't know. And the people that we do know are people that have already seen us in a different light or at our worst. So any out of the way behavior is par for the course for them. But what's also interesting is sometimes, our internet following is only getting half the story as well. Sometimes we'll show them our wild and untamed side, but they never see the side of us that shouts hallelujah on Sundays. And what's even more confusing is when we do show all sides on the net. Now, all of us are confused because we'll thank God for waking us up in one post and then curse out our ex and whoever they're dating now in the next post.

It's amazing how the internet can mirror the Christian community. While I understand that none of us are the same all the time, should the differences be so drastic? Should it really be like night and day? This is a problem when it comes to people seeing God in us. Often times, we show them one side of ourselves on Sunday morning, but by Sunday night, they see something completely different from us. We're treating church as though it was our own personal internet and the persona that we show there isn't real.

There's a phrase that's often thrown around: "Keep it real". Now, I've got my own phrase when it comes to that: "Real is a relative term". Simply put, what's real to me may not be real to you, and vice versa. Real is relative to who you are, your experiences and how you see life. What I'm finding these days is it's hard to find anyone that really keeps it real. People will say things behind your back that they'd never say to your face. People will represent themselves to be something that they're really not. People will get on the internet and be something that they're really not. And people will say that they love you when they really don't.

We've still yet to learn that we can't serve two masters. We have one foot in the world and one foot in The Word. We must understand that we can sing and shout all we want in service. We can profess our love for The Lord and our fellow man all we want when we're in service. We can shake hands during the fellowship hour and hug one another like we love one another after communion all we want. What we do to one another on Sundays just doesn't matter. Because the reality is, how we'd treat each other from Monday through Saturday is who we really are.

As I stated, an alternate universe, though not real, can affect your reality. Meaning, if your Sunday morning persona is not real and more like your internet persona, then it will change the way I view you during the rest of the week when I see the real you. You'll say "God bless you", but I won't know if you really mean it. You'll say "I'm saved", but I won't know if you really are. You'll say "I love you", but I won't know if you really do.

This week, let's redefine what's really real in our lives. This isn't a call to be perfect, as none of us are. But it's more in line with what I wrote in my last book, *Peace In My Mind*. It's a call to find a way to bring your physical and spiritual selves together. As I stated, we can't serve two masters and I think that we struggle because we try to. As it is with the internet, we get wild and out of control because we've convinced ourselves that that's what we're supposed to do when we're there. After all, that's what everyone else is doing, right? And no one's watching anyway, right?

It's so similar to what we do outside of the sanctuary. We're on our best behavior in church because all of the other Christians are watching and somehow, we've foolishly convinced ourselves that that's the only time God is watching. But once the benediction is given, we log off God's high speed connection and log into what the world has to offer. But all you need to know is that God is the ultimate behavior modifier. Omnipotent and omnipresent. You can lie on the net and you can lie in church, but God knows the truth. And no matter what you think you're doing in secret, someone is always watching.

If you didn't come to praise Him, why are you here?

[30]Ye shall keep my Sabbaths and reverence my sanctuary; I am the Lord
— Leviticus 19:30

We have to take a break from the norm this week so that I can deliver a message that I think we all need. This week's email is one that I shouldn't have to write. It's a message that we shouldn't need, but we always do. It's like one of those lessons that our parents try to teach us over and over and over again, but we seem to show a refusal to learn. And because of that, we seem to get no better. It's time for all of the "church folk" to get out of the church so that Christians can be about the business of praising God.

For some reason, we have decided that we own the church. No longer are we in God's house. Like an overpaid, overhyped professional athlete, we seem to be saying "this is MY house!" No longer are we of the mindset of "that's my church home", we're now of the mindset of "that's MY church". Is it really? When Jesus died, did He not rise again and leave you in charge? I'm so sure that's not the case.

But there are some among us that feel that because they dress better than anyone else in the congregation, they run the church. There are some among us that feel that because they can sing like nobody's business or can play church songs until we all shout in the aisles, they run God's house. And for some reason, there are those among us that feel as if they can just be loud and disrespectful and that should be enough to get their way in the sanctuary. Well, I have a bit of news. No matter how many of us stride back and forth during service so that we can be seen, there are no runways in church. No matter what kind of "performance" we give each Sunday, this isn't a talent show. And no matter how loud we feel the need to be so that our voice can be heard, we're not at some backyard barbeque. This is church and all that's not done to the glory of God is done in vain.

For some reason, we have decided that we don't need to adhere to the principles of Christianity any longer. We sit back and we wonder why the world has the view of the church that it does. We've become judgmental about those that don't choose to worship with us. We call them sinners and wayward souls, as though we are above reproach and don't share some of the same ills that society has. Maybe it's time we took the stained glass windows out of the church and put up mirrors instead. This message has been sent over and over again, but it obviously bears repeating. Just because you were submerged in water, doesn't mean you've been born again. Just because you show up every Sunday, doesn't mean you're a Christian.

If you're unaware of what's expected, then allow me to shed some light. Every time you're in church, you're in church! Christianity and Christian behavior doesn't end with the benediction on Sunday. It should extend through the week. It should extend to choir rehearsal. It should extend to the usher board meeting. It should extend to the church business meeting. Church is not about "showtime", it's about God's time. We aren't supposed to only be Christians when the stage lights come up. It's a full time, 24-hour a day, 7 days a week job. And just like any other job, if you can't perform to what the job requires, you need a new job. But rather than that, as a Christian, I'd rather we get more training so that we can be better at our jobs.

This week, take something different when you go into the church doors. Don't take your attitude. Don't take your sense of entitlement. Don't take your feeling that church doesn't start until you show up and it ends the moment you leave. Don't take your sense that nothing will ever work unless you're calling the shots. Don't take a sense that your song is the only one worth singing on Sunday morning. And above all, don't take an attitude that suggests that not only are you the only one that will make it to Heaven, but God will make you gatekeeper and you will decide whether we get in or not. The only thing you need to come with is Jesus. Anything less than that is no longer needed. We have to get back to the business of serving God. It's time for the "church folk" to leave the church so the Christians can worship in peace.

Patience on God's highway

*14The seeds that fell among the thorns represent those who hear the
message, but all too quickly the message is crowded out by the cares and
riches and pleasures of this life. And so they never grow into maturity.
15And the seeds that fell on the good soil represent honest, good-hearted
people who hear God's word, cling to it, and patiently produce a huge
harvest. – Luke 8:14-15*

Have you ever been in a traffic jam on the freeway? Drives you
crazy, right? Especially when it's during a time of day when
there should be no traffic beyond the norm. You immediately
start looking for an exit so that you can get to an alternate
route. As things normally go, you get into the right lane so that
you can exit ASAP. But what happens then? The sign says that
the exit you're seeking is only a half mile away, but it may as
well be a million miles away because everyone else has the same
bright idea and that right lane is full and slowly moving.

All of a sudden, the song you were just jamming to
doesn't feel like the jam anymore. The food you were on your
way to eat doesn't seem as appealing anymore. That feeling of
joy that you felt from finally being off work and on your way
home is no longer there. You are officially stuck in a place that
you'd rather not be in and you're frustrated because as of this
moment, there's nothing you can do about it. But in reality,
there is something you can do.

If you've ever been in this position, you know what
often happens next. You wait and you creep and you wait and
you creep, and soon, you reach that elusive exit. Now, you'll
finally get off this dreaded highway and get on to where you
were going and back to whatever place of happiness you were
in your mind. But something strange happens.

As soon as you get near your exit, the traffic clears right
where you were trying to get off. Maybe there was an accident,
maybe there was brief construction, maybe there was a car

pulled over by a trooper or maybe someone's car broke down. Whatever the case, your normal traffic resumes and you no longer need that detour you thought you needed. After all, who knows what drama may have been waiting on that alternate route today? All you need to do is stay on your normal route and you'll be home safely in no time. Music is sounding good again, you've got your appetite back, and driving 60 to 70mph (80 to 85 for you speeders out there) never felt so good. It's amazing what a little patience, whether exercised or forced upon us, can do.

This reminds me of how things can sometimes go within our lives. On occasion, it can seem as if everything is clogging our lanes as we're on the way to our destination. We know where we wanna go, we know what's waiting on the other side of that traffic and we know how bad we wanna get there for whatever reasons we have. But too often we find ourselves seduced by that alternate route. We find ourselves wanting to hurry to find what we feel has already been promised to us. But as the saying goes, what God has for you is for you. If you believe that to be true, what's your hurry?

Sometimes, we're exactly where we're supposed to be in life. It may not be where you want to be, but it may be where you're supposed to be at that moment in time. There could be something that you're meant to learn from this situation before things open up for you. This place in your life could be a destination on the way to another destination. Or maybe we haven't quite worked hard enough to be where we think we ought to be in life and we need to recommit ourselves. Maybe you're in this place at this moment to be protected from moving too fast. There could be real danger ahead on this freeway of life that's being cleared out right now in order for you to proceed. All that's required of you is to be patient and wait for a sign. If this road is to be closed, you'll find out soon enough. And instead of you having to seek an alternate route on your own because you just can't wait, one will be provided for you. In the meantime, turn up the radio and relax.

This week, dust off your patience and put it to good use. Often, we fail to work for the results that we want in our lives. I see this way too often in my people. We want everything and we're willing to do nothing to get it. We won't get up in the morning at a decent hour, but we want someone to hire us. We won't work the jobs that we're given to the absolute best of our God-given abilities, but we want to be promoted. We can't work a 9 to 5 properly, but we expect to run companies one day.

We expect God to reward us with earthly blessings and Heaven when we die, and yet we fail to do His work while we're here. When we finally commit to doing the work that is necessary for success, we fail to be patient, refusing to understand that some results are not automatic. Even though we've planned our route home, understand that there may be traffic on the way. Some results take time. Some results require…patience. Take your time. He never closes one door without opening another. That goes for freeways, too.

Week of November 1, 2009

Are you working with God?

*[20]But wilt thou know, O vain man, that faith without works is dead? –
James 2:20
(Also read James 2:14-19)*

Something that I often try to get across to people is the idea
that if you're working together with someone on something,
it'll never be successful if you're not all pulling in the same
direction. I struggle with this daily on my job, but it doesn't just
exist in that setting. This is true in love, it's true in friendship
and it's critical in family. But most importantly, it's true in our
spirituality. However, what I've been hearing a lot lately are
people in defense mode. Whether I'm overhearing
conversation, reading posts on Facebook or whatever, the
general theme seems to be "don't judge me because God is
working with me". A true sentiment indeed, but that's only half
the equation.

In reality, God is working with each and every one of
us, even the people that we often feel aren't living right. But in
the confines of that work, where does our responsibility lie?
While God is working with us, what is our responsibility? What
concerns me is that we usually pull the "God is working with
me" card when we're at our worst. And while there's nothing
wrong with that in theory, I question why we do it when we're
at our worst because we chose to be at our worst as opposed to
pulling it out when certain circumstances and situations may
have brought out the worst in us.

If you catch us in service, we're model Christians. No
one says "Amen" louder than we do, no one sings to His glory
the way we do and no one prays at His throne quite like we do.
However, if you catch us outside those church walls, no one
drinks and parties like we do, no one smokes like we do, no
one swears like we do and unfortunately, no one makes excuses
and justifications for their behavior like we do.

If you dare to call us out on this, not just because you think we're wrong, but based on who we claimed we were and how we claim to be saved, we'll tell you one of three things: "Don't judge me", "You're not perfect either" or…that's right, "God is working with me". I can tell you what a mighty work God is doing in my life on Sunday, but if you see me on Friday when the ways of the world are doing a mighty work on me, you better not say a word to me about it or I'll have some words to say to you. Strangely, we seem to want to embrace our imperfection when in the midst of our most imperfect behavior.

Unfortunately, as soon as we lose our poise and start to display some less than positive behavior, that's exactly when the world seems to be watching. The first line of defense is to defend. We downplay the significance of what we're doing. "I used that language because they pushed my buttons and I was upset". "I didn't plan to get drunk or high, but it was just one night. It was a party and we were just having fun".

The problem that exists with "saved people" is that we think we have an understanding with God that we actually don't because only we understand why we continue on the path that we're on. While God is aware of our behavior and even knows what we'll do before we do it, it doesn't mean that He understands why we claim to have turned our lives over to Him, but we continue to do the same things that we did before. As the saved, we continue to do all of the things we did in the world, but we somehow think because we're "saved", we're good because we know enough to repent.

We have to get to the point where we understand that spirituality isn't a security blanket. It's supposed to be a way of life. It's not something to fall back on when you've done wrong. It's not a crutch to help you limp through a life of sin. It's the strength to help you walk through life with your head held high, knowing that you're trying to live right daily and not just when it suits you. We have to get ourselves to a point where we're not trying to take advantage of God, as if such a thing is possible. The God we serve is so loving, He created us with a free will. You can do as you please in this life as long as you can stand the consequences of your actions. And if God wanted to make you live right every day, He could. But it is His desire that you will choose to live right as opposed to being forced to. And while we'll all sin and fall short from time to time, He is willing to forgive our trespasses. The ones we commit purposely and otherwise.

This week, don't wait for someone else to question your commitment. Look yourself in the mirror and question it for yourself. And before you react in anger at what's being said about you, have the courage to ask yourself if it's true. I've talked in these emails before about having a relationship with God. Now, having written a book based on relationships, I'd like to think I know one or two things about them. The most successful ones are based on give and take. That doesn't mean that one person does all the giving while the other one does all the taking. Both parties have to be willing to do both.

You can't just give God those 3 or 4 hours that you give Him every Sunday morning and just take His love, kindness and forgiveness for the rest of the week. More is required of us. One foot in the world and one in Christianity won't do. It's alright to be a work in progress as long as you're working towards something. Yes, no one should judge you when your behavior is less than stellar because God is working with you. The question is, are you working with Him?

Week of November 8, 2009

The blessing in leadership

[20]I lead in the way of righteousness, in the midst of the paths of judgment. [21]That I may cause those that love me to inherit substance... – Proverbs 8:20-21

Last week on my job, I decided that I needed to be even more focused than I usually try to be daily, and I'm pretty focused on the job. I'm focused to the point where I irritate my employees because I expect them to have that same focus and intensity that I have so that we can all be great at what we do. As a Black man in an office that's primarily Black, I think it's important for me to set that example. I want to prove that contrary to popular belief, hard working Black men do exist.

However, I have to admit that when my employees don't seem to be on my level, I get irritated and it shows. While I simply want to inspire greatness by showing that I'm willing to work just as hard as I expect them to, it doesn't always work. What that requires is an adjustment in me so that I don't lose perspective. I have to get used to the fact that everyone doesn't share my passion and that's okay.

Great leaders are what we need in this life, and everyday that I wake up, I want to be great. That's my goal in whatever I choose to do in life. Whether the job seems lowly or not is no longer the point. Whether you're the janitor or the CEO, the secretary or the boss, the teacher or the student, the author or his subject, you should aspire to be great at what you do. But in order to inspire greatness, great leadership must first be in place.

At the same time, we all have to understand that we're all at different stages in life. Some of us are at different levels and we will perform as such. Sometimes, it's not a matter of right and wrong or better or worse. It just means that we're in different places. If we're not aware of this, it can cause problems. For example, the most successful entertainers and athletes in the world are successful because they possess a drive and focus that others just don't have. That's what makes them great. That's why they stand out. That's why they are who they are. That kind of focus isn't given to all of us or we'd all be singing, dancing, running, jumping or whatever. But that's okay. We weren't all destined to be doing the same things. Some of us are meant to walk a different, less intense path in life.

While we do have to acknowledge that everyone doesn't see the world, work or life in the same way that we do, we have to remember that some don't see it that way because no one has ever shown them the way. This is especially true in the spiritual community. In the spiritual community, the art of education has gone missing. We don't teach anymore, especially in the Black church. We'd much rather judge and attempt to reprimand. We've decided not to teach those that don't know, but rather put them down for not knowing. We've decided that we don't want to be hard working examples of how we're supposed to live, but rather the unofficial gatekeepers of the Kingdom. We've decided to criticize the pastor for what we perceive as wrongdoing, as opposed to taking our concerns to him directly so that he may be allowed to explain his actions before we run off and begin gossiping.

God has placed some of us in certain positions in life for a reason. Some of us are in leadership positions because we have something to offer to those that we're charged to lead. Some of us aren't placed in leadership roles because we still have something to learn before we can effectively teach and lead someone else. Those of us that are blessed to be at higher levels in life should always be seeking to bring others up to our level. Conversely, those of us that are at lower levels in life should not only be willing to rise to the next level, but we should be willing to accept that assistance of those that are trying to help us. If you're not receptive to what someone else is trying to teach you, then you could miss out on a blessing. While there's greatness in leadership, there can also be greatness in those that choose to follow the example of great leadership.

This week, evaluate your position in life. If you've been placed in a leadership position, whether it be on the job, in the home or in the sanctuary, lead to the best of your ability. Start by being an example of what you expect of others. Don't place requirements on others that you couldn't live up to if you had to. Use your position to teach. Use your position to inspire. Use your position to motivate.

Only the selfish are looking to go to the top alone. If you don't wake up each day expecting to see greatness when you look in the mirror, then you're missing what God has for you. We are already great. We just have to be willing to reach our potential. No matter where you are, what you do or where you come from, you can achieve greatness with the right effort. Jesus is your example. He was just a lowly carpenter's son. Look at what He accomplished.

How are you livin'?

35Heaven and earth shall pass away, but my words shall not pass away
36But of that day and hour knoweth no man, no, not the angels of Heaven,
but my Father only – Matthew 24:35-36

If you knew for a fact that you were dying, what would you do? How would you feel? Would you be afraid? Would you be regretful? Would you be pleased with how you lived your life? Would you be looking forward to the afterlife? Better yet, how would you approach your last days? Where would you go? What would you do? How much would your life change? How differently would you live your last days in comparison to how you're living right now? Tough questions, for sure. Do you have the answers?

While I hate to bombard you with questions on Sunday morning, these are questions that we need to answer from time to time. Are you ready to die right now? Have you gotten all that you can out of life? Have you done all that you've been assigned to do here on earth? Have you forgiven everyone that you were supposed to forgive? Have you asked for forgiveness from those that you've done wrong? Have you taken all of the opportunities that you've been given to make right out of the wrong in your life, whatever that may be? Or did you assume that you had time. Or better yet, did you just assume that it would work out somehow. I wonder.

Too often, we approach life as though we have all the time in the world. We approach life as though there's never a sense of urgency necessary. But every now and then, something happens that reminds us that we won't be here forever. As my Pastor has said from the pulpit before, we assume that we'll keep going to everyone else's funeral and no one will ever have to come to ours. So why is it that when we have those moments of clarity about life being short, the first thing that we want to do is "live it up"? Why is it that when those moments come along, the first thing we want to do is go out and live with some sort of excitement before we die? Now, I'm not against living a life of fun and excitement, but why don't we ever look to live right?

We place unnecessary stress on ourselves by not doing today what we should've done yesterday. We're so busy "living for the moment" and "living life to the fullest because tomorrow isn't promised" that we're forgetting that we should be living *right* for the moment because tomorrow isn't promised. We forget that part of our living to the fullest should include being the best that we can be. I'm not here to tell anyone what any of this entails. No matter what we believe or don't believe, we all have our own set of morals and values. We all have a sense of what we feel is right and wrong. And we're all guilty of failing to live up to those standards at times and acting as though we're unaware that we're not at our best.

This week, come to a realization now and adjust your life accordingly. News flash: You are dying! All of us are. Whether you're sick or well, in the hospital or at home, living right or not. It will happen and there's no way of knowing when. Plenty have come back from the so-called brink of death to out live those that appeared healthier than they were. It is appointed of man once to die. You can't avoid it and neither can I. You're leaving here. But what you do while you're here will live on forever. And while we'd all plan as many trips and nights of fun that we could if we knew our exact expiration date, somewhere in the mix we should all consider someone else. If there's a fractured relationship, repair it. If there's a change that needs to be made in your life, make it. If you haven't lived up to what God has predestined for you, you may wanna get started.

This is not meant to be as dire as it sounds, but we need to value our lives and the relationships that we have a little bit more than the material possessions that we aspire to have so often. The fact that tomorrow isn't promised shouldn't always be used as an excuse for reckless behavior. It should be used as a reminder that we need to treat one another a lot better than we do. It should be used as a reminder that we were meant to do more than hold grudges. It should be used as a reminder that we should always be looking to treat others as we wish to be treated. It should be used as a reminder that we shouldn't let our disagreements divide us for years and years and years.

If we can't come to some common ground, agree to disagree and move on. Yes, life is too short and love is too plentiful not to be sharing it. Death doesn't always fire a warning shot. You could be lying on your death bed when you go to sleep tonight. But if we're doing this right, we won't concern ourselves so much with how we may die. We'll concern ourselves with how we live.

Week of December 6, 2009

There, but for the grace of God…

⁴But God, who is rich in mercy, for his great love wherewith He loved us,
⁵Even when we were dead in sins, hath quickened us (made us alive)
together with Christ, (by grace ye are saved) – Ephesians 2:4-5

This past week, we saw the covers pulled back on another
famous person's life. We all sat back and saw secrets revealed
that proved that he wasn't what a lot of people thought he was.
While I once again found it sad that we could spend hours
upon hours on news channels talking about Tiger Woods
cheating on his wife when we're sending more troops off to
war, unemployment is still rising and we still haven't solved
health care in this country, I couldn't help but think that this is
a referendum on who we are as people and where our priorities
lie. And while I'm not completely sure what makes us think that
we really know people that we have no personal interaction
with, it made me wonder about us. Are any of us all that we
appear to be?

When our athletes and celebrities fall short, we usually
react with disappointment and hurt feelings. I understand this
on a small scale. When you choose to follow someone, support
their gift or whatever, you'd like to believe that they're
reasonably good people. You'd like to believe they're morally
sound. You wanna trust them. However, when we find out that
they're human just like we are, why do we slip into judgment?
Why do we let anger take a hold of us? And most importantly,
why do we react in disappointment to the fact that they're not
what we thought they were, as if we're all that we want people
to think we are?

For all of us, there's a public persona and a private
persona. That doesn't mean that one is good and one is evil,
one is dark and the other is light or anything like that. It just
means that there's often a side of us that we allow the public to
see and a side that we keep private. In short, we all put our best

foot forward. But if you're ever going to take a step in life, then you must know that at some point, your worst foot will be revealed. Would you like to be judged by all when that happens? I don't think so.

What's interesting to me is the idea that when someone falls, we look at them skeptically from this day forward, as if to say "I don't even know who you are anymore". But we must be careful when looking down our nose at another. When I see others looking to condemn, I often wonder where they've been in their lives and were they always living right. Of course not.

If it weren't for God's grace, we'd all be exposed daily. We go to work everyday with people that we don't like, and some of us are just as fake as we can be with them. We shake hands each Sunday after service with people that we'll be talking about over Sunday dinner. We hug people in our own family that we have issues with that haven't been resolved. In short, all of us are capable of being disingenuous. All of us are capable of pretending to be something other than what we truly are.

What's also quite interesting is the fact that we always seem to know where someone else has gone wrong, but we have to be told where we went wrong. And even after being told, we're still resistant to the information. We spend so much time in someone else's business and so little time on our own lives that we don't know when we're off track. We spend so much time trying to put someone else in check that we have no idea where we're headed. We're so caught up in someone else's seemingly failing relationship that we can't even repair our own. We're so busy running around singing about "the God in me" that we're not even remembering just how flawed we all are.

This week, try something different. When you see someone fall from their supposed glory, whether famous or otherwise, don't waste your energy being judge, jury and executioner. Try praying for them. While your opinion on the local talk shows and around the gossip circles at work may be quite valuable to those that listen, I guarantee you that your prayers for the individual will do far more good. While I understand the desire to wanna condemn another's behavior, maybe support is what's needed. Understand that you can support an individual without supporting their behavior. Understand that we all have demons, but some of us are fortunate enough to have them remain private. But most of all, understand that someday, the shoe may be on the other foot.

Are you really brand new?

[1]I beseech you therefore, brethren, by the mercies of God, that ye present your bodies as a living sacrifice, holy, acceptable unto God, which is your reasonable service [2]And be not conformed to this world: but be ye transformed by the renewing of your mind... – Romans 12:1-2

We have a New Year's Eve service every year at my church. While most churches will have a service on New Year's Eve that starts before midnight and carries over into the New Year, we have ours early in the evening so the members can get home before all the senseless gunfire of the night starts. We're able to gather together, sing songs, testify, pray and get home before 9pm. In a way, it's also like an accommodation for those that are conflicted about how they should bring in the New Year. Should you be praying or should you be partying? You can't be two places at the same time, right? Well, problem solved. You can go to service and toast the New Year. Or so it would seem.

What I find interesting is the fact that even with the early start time, we still can't fill up our church on New Year's Eve. Not even a third of our Sunday morning congregation was there. Even with all of the partiers having time to pray before they play, they still don't show. Even with the church being accommodating and not making you choose between the church and the club, the club still wins by a landslide. It's like a microcosm of our lives. God wants a life of service from us, but will settle for just 10% of our time and finances, and we still struggle to do that. Why is that?

As it is so often, we hear people talking about change for the New Year. "Brand new year, brand new me" is what they say. We remain unaware that you can claim brand new year, brand new me all you want, but if you ended this last year like you've ended all the others, how much change can you really expect at midnight? We're still failing to realize that life is about constant evolution. Life is about constant change, not just yearly inventory.

If I don't hear the brand new me scenario, I hear a lot of people speaking about wanting the year to end so that they can start fresh. There's always a lot of talk about wanting new things for themselves in the next year. However, what I never hear about is how much we're going to do for someone else in the New Year. We've talked about this before in these emails. If you really want to be blessed, at some point, you're gonna have to bless someone else. We're so used to focusing on ourselves that we can't bear to focus on someone else. But as I stated in the earlier paragraphs, we won't even sacrifice a few hours of our New Year's celebration for God, so it stands to reason that we wouldn't sacrifice for one another, right?

What I think is happening is that we've still failed to take God seriously. We've failed to take our lives seriously. While God is constantly bending and twisting for us, we never make any concessions for Him. We still operate as though we have forever to get right with God. We treat God like we treat relationships. We party and play our youth away, but when we're tired and worn out, we wanna settle down into a nice little forever after. As if God doesn't have any use for the youthful and energized you.

People are still trying to blow us up on planes and we don't realize how close to the end we are. Instead of realizing how God has spared our lives, we're so busy focusing on what went wrong for us in the last year, all the while ignoring what went right for us. We talk about how we can't wait until the New Year comes so that things can get better for us, but maybe it's time for something different. Maybe it's time for a renewed mind. Maybe it's time for a little appreciation. We have no idea how blessed we truly are. Maybe it's time to share those blessings with others.

This week, re-evaluate your New Year's makeover. Instead of making this year about all that we want to do for ourselves, why not make it about what we'll do for others? Maybe the way to fulfillment is in doing for others. Maybe this year should be about sacrifice. Maybe we'll have a more enriched year if we plan to do for others, including God, instead of making so many plans to do for ourselves. Make this year more about a spiritual connection rather than a love connection or a financial connection. And if you must fall in love with someone, fall in love with God first. Follow that up by loving yourself. Do this and I assure you that everything else will fall into place.

Spreading The Word in the name of love, not fear

[5]I am the Lord, and there is none else, there is no God beside me: I girded (equipped) thee, though thou hast not known me: [6]That they may know from the rising of the sun, and from the west, that there is none beside me. I am the Lord, and there is none else. [7]I form the light, and create darkness: I make peace, and create evil: I the Lord do all these things – Isaiah 45:5-7

With everything that happens on a day to day basis in our world, we all need to be reminded that there is still hope. When a situation like Haiti happens, we need to remember that God is still in charge. In times like these, people will often lean on their faith to get them through. Those that don't believe become more aware that there is something greater than they are in the world.

So when people need something to believe in the most, it would seem to me that the men of God that stand in the pulpits should be more open to spreading a message of hope. It would seem to me that we as Christians would do more to spread a message of hope. We should be more open to spreading the message that though lives may be lost, God is still saving lives. While there are many of us that hold to that philosophy, there are some of us that look to capitalize on the fears of the people.

Now, I'm not suggesting that these types of things shouldn't make you more aware that your time here isn't forever. What I am suggesting is that when things like this happen, we should implore people to seek God because it's the right thing to do, and not because God is some big bad wolf coming to blow their houses down. We should implore people to seek God because it enables you to handle things like this a little better when you do know God. Those that don't know Him will look at catastrophes with a sense of hopelessness because they don't realize that Jesus gave us hope. But maybe that's our fault. Maybe people don't know the hope we have in Jesus because we're delivering a different message.

Our ministers and our churches have to get out of the condemnation business right now and get back into the business of leading people to Christ. Our ministers and our churches have to get back into the business of assisting God in saving souls and not proclaiming who's going to hell and who's going to heaven. Whether you're a pastor or a bench member, you have no heaven or hell to put anyone into. We must get back to leaving all judgments to God because we're not pure enough to administer any Christian justice. When we get caught up in playing God, we lose every time.

When we have ministers that claim to know which entertainers are demon possessed and are going to hell, but they don't even know who's demon possessed in their own congregation, we have a problem. When you can deliver a message from your pulpit that suggests we either need to turn off our iPods or go to hell, but you don't even know half the members of your congregation, thus, you don't know them well enough to know their hearts, we have a problem.

If we put more effort into fixing our own families and our own congregations, we wouldn't have to worry about what people are doing in the entertainment industry. But instead, we have "ministers" like Pat Robertson, who displayed his God complex again this week when he suggested that the situation in Haiti was brought on by that country's "pact with the devil". If the message being delivered from the so called man of God is that every natural disaster that happens in the world is the result of a deal with the devil or God being angry because we're all so evil, who's the real threat to me?

The church has to understand that fear is not a motivator and we must stop using it to gain a profit. Support my ministry or go to hell isn't what we're supposed to be about. This is the time when we need to be expressing the goodness of God. It's so easy to fall into Armageddon mode when disaster strikes, but we must also remember what's good in our lives.

When things like Haiti happen, we need to be more appreciative of life. We can't see this as an opportunity to instill fear in everyone. We can't take this as a sign that Jesus will be here next week. This is God's work and we shouldn't try and exalt ourselves by claiming to understand it all. As we preach the rapture, we must remember that the Bible tells us that we know not the day nor the hour that the end will come. Just because we've seen natural disasters more frequently these days doesn't mean that any one of us can figure out what God plans to do. A lot of us will still pass through the graveyard before God comes back.

This week, instead of spreading a message of fear, try spreading a message of love. Try spreading the notion that Jesus wants you to accept Him as your Savior because it's good to know Him, and not because you think the world is coming to an end. We all like to walk around telling everyone that we don't have much longer here, but the reality is we have as much time as God says we have, and none of us knows how much that is. So show someone the benefits of living right just because life is better when you do and not because you think Jesus is on your block. Show someone that God is good because He is, and not because you could've been in Haiti last week. He's good because no matter where you are or what you're facing in life, He's still blessing you.

Week of January 24, 2010

If you can't trust God, who can you trust?

[1] They that trust in the Lord shall be as Mount Zion, which cannot be removed, but abideth forever – Psalm 125:1

Everyday on my job, I have to ask at least one of my employees "Do you trust me"? I wanna know if they trust me to put them in positions to succeed. They always tell me "Yes". After they tell me yes, they immediately follow that up by doing the opposite of what I asked them to do. Not because they're insubordinate or hard headed or anything like that. Usually, it's because they can't see as far down the road as I can. They can't see the end result of what I'm asking them to do. Because they can't see it, they're hesitant to do it. Thus, they don't trust me as much as they say they do or as much as they may think they do.

The same thing has happened in my relationships. Whether it be relationships in the romantic sense or in the friendship sense, I've been told that I am trustworthy. I've been told that I can be counted on and that I never let people down. Whether it's a shoulder to cry on, advice or just being there, I do my best to be there for those that I care about. However, it seems that when people ask me for something, they seem to want to check on me from time to time to see if I'm going to keep my word *this time* or if I'm going to let them down. Interesting. That doesn't sound like a lot of trust to me.

Now this kind of behavior, though frustrating to me, is just a part of life. People are filled with doubt. It's sometimes difficult for us to trust one another. I just have to deal with the fact that people won't always trust me as much as I think they should, no matter what I've done or shown them in the past. That's okay because I'm just Kelly. I'm just a man. These are not life or death situations we're talking about. No one is required to trust me in order to survive. It's just one of those things.

Where this doesn't make sense is where God is concerned. Trusting man and trusting God couldn't be more opposite. It's not even close to being the same thing. And yet, I find that we do treat them the same. Let me ask you a question: When has God ever failed you? The answer is never. And if you have enough vision to look further down the road, He never will. This is the key to a better life here on earth and eternal life when we leave here. And remember, as we often discuss in these emails, just because God doesn't do what you want Him to or answer you when you want to be answered doesn't mean that He has forsaken you or let you down. But if we were always aware of that, I wouldn't be writing this email, would I?

We often like to throw around the phrase "When someone shows you who they are, believe them". While that's very, very true, what I've found is that we're too often using that phrase in a negative sense. This phrase has some positives to it as well. If someone shows you the good that's in them, you can believe that, too. If someone shows you that they can be trusted, you can believe that as well. I've also found that you shouldn't assume someone's gonna do you wrong until they actually do. While it may be difficult to apply some of these principles to man, all of these things we should apply to God. I'm confident that you've never given a problem to God, and I mean really and truly turned it over to Him, that He didn't work out for you. The first time He lets you down, that's when you should start questioning Him. But I gotta let you know, you'll be waiting a while for that one.

This week, not only learn to give your fellow man the benefit of the doubt, if you've found yourself doubting God, give Him another shot. I know it's hard to just trust someone from time to time, especially in this day and age of backstabbing and selling out, but if a person has never done you wrong, given you bad advice or led you astray, where is the mistrust coming from? Is it possible that there are some things within you that can't be trusted? Are you afraid to give your trust in a given situation because you know that you couldn't be trusted to do the right thing if the situation was reversed? Just something to think about.

I think this is why we sometimes have a problem trusting God. We know that the blessings that we're asking for, we sometimes don't deserve. We know that even though we're asking God to do right by us, we're not always doing right by Him. The best thing about all of this is we serve a God that will bless us in spite of our faults. He will bless us in spite of our shortcomings. He will bless us even when we haven't been our best and we don't deserve what we're asking for. Unlike man, He won't hold grudges. Unlike man, He won't disappoint you. Unlike man, He's always worth the benefit of any doubt that you have in you. He's shown you who He is. You should believe Him.

Week of February 21, 2010

This misconception in unconditional support

*[17] A friend is always loyal, and a brother is born to help in time of need –
Proverbs 17:17 (New Living Translation)*

As I was writing my first book, *Temporarily Disconnected*, I found
myself stopping at certain points to wonder who would care
about what I had to say. I wondered would it make a difference
in anyone's life. All the reasons for me writing the book were
valid. I saw some things in the Black community as far as
families and relationships that I wanted to see change. I was
dating people that I felt had issues. I had issues that I didn't
realize that I had.

But most important, I saw some things in our young
people, especially in my own family, that needed to be
corrected. I was saying a lot of things in that book that people
needed to hear, but didn't necessarily want to hear. But I felt it
was necessary. I felt it was my place to say something to my
people. This was my way of supporting my community. I know
that it had an effect on some that read it. But what do you do
when you've hit *a* target, but not *the* target? What do you do
when you're talking all day and all night and while someone
heard you, the message didn't necessarily reach the ears it was
intended to reach?

One of the hardest things we'll ever have to do in life is
to try and teach someone that doesn't wanna be taught. If you
have kids, you know this one all too well. No matter what, our
kids are always smarter than we are. And if they're not, they
know someone who is and are willing to follow what they say
as long as that person is telling them what they wanna hear.
Forgetting all along that at the first sign of real trouble, they'll
have to come crawling back to us know nothing parents to bail
them out of whatever jam they may find themselves in. And
what about those adults in our lives that we wish to teach?
Your friends, significant others, siblings or whatever can be just

as challenging as those kids. Well, whether it's appreciated or not, we sometimes have to support one another anyway. But there's a trick to it that I don't think we always understand.

The biggest misconception I see when it comes to support is we believe that to support someone, you must stand by them "no matter what". Sounds good in a song or a movie, but in real life, this thinking is incorrect. If I love you and I support you, I must be willing to tell you when you're right *and* when you're wrong. In the event that you're wrong, I must be willing to take no part in your wrongdoing in order to prove my support.

If you love someone, you can't be willing to aid them in making a mistake. You can't sit back and support something that you know will fall apart on the premise that you'll be there when it does to help heal the situation. You can be a part of the rebuilding efforts without taking part in the destruction. Sometimes people need support and sometimes they need the truth, and a lot of the times, the two aren't the same. Think of all of the pain and heartache you could save that person by speaking out before they screw things up. As I learned when writing that first book, say what you have to say anyway. You never know when they might listen to you.

Look at it spiritually. If you're reading this email and you're of the Christian faith, you understand that God loves and supports us. But He doesn't support everything that we do. He's not fond of our fighting, our backstabbing, our sins or anything like that. And He has said so in His Word. Does it mean that He loves us any less if He won't support us "no matter what", as we so often wish of one another? Does it mean that He loves us any less because He not only doesn't endorse our wrongdoing in this life, but He wants no part of it? No, it doesn't. It's because He loves and supports us that He tells us when we're wrong. In an effort to spare us the heartache and pain that comes with living outside of His will, He tells us where we're wrong and refuses to roll with us if we insist on continuing on that path. That's real support. That's real love. Yes, there is no friend like Jesus.

This week, redefine what it means to give your support to someone. If you see someone on the wrong path, do what you can to redirect them. If they won't listen, try something different. Try being a living example of what you hope to see in them. Just remember, unless we're talking about your minor children here, they really don't have to listen to you. But supporting their mistakes doesn't make you a great friend, brother, sister, father, mother or relative. Helping them to see them does. Agreeing to disagree does. Loving them enough to not take part in something that will be destructive in their lives does. If they see you as a true friend, your opinion matters whether you agree or disagree. And while this may cause some discomfort at the time, any real friendship should be able to survive it. Just think of how many times Jesus has taken us back when we disagreed with Him.

Are you on God's program?

Read Leviticus 19:30

When it comes to dishonesty, there has to be only one thing worse than someone lying to you. That has to be when we both know that you're lying to me, we both know that we both know, and you continue to lie to me. Possibly in hopes that I will be convinced to believe the lie. Possibly in hopes that the lie will somehow become true. Whatever the reason, it makes no sense to continue the charade. Either change or move on. This is the state of our churches today. And I imagine this is the position that a lot of us find ourselves in with God. Some of us are trying to fool someone that already knows the truth, when He'd rather we change or move on.

If you go to any church on a regular basis, then you frequently witness people playing church. You witness people coming through the doors with no real intention on serving God and every intention on bringing soap opera-type drama into the sanctuary on a weekly basis. If you don't know any better, it's hard to tell everyone apart. People that don't treat their children right shout louder and longer than anyone in church every Sunday. People that talk about the Pastor behind his back instead of praying for him can quote Bible verses to you on cue. At the same time, these folks have every intention on changing the order of service every time they show up. All the while failing to understand that when we enter the sanctuary, whether we know it or not, we are on God's program.

For many of us, the church has become like the playground was when we were children. We want every game played our way or we're unhappy. And in the event that something doesn't go our way, we wanna take our ball and go home. Well, if you're unwilling to play well with others, the going home is encouraged. But know this, there is no one here on this earth that can stop God's program. This goes for everyone from Pastor to usher.

We must remember that while we are *on* God's program, we are not God's program. Simply put, whether you like it or not, the church will go on without you. The moment we decide somewhere in our minds that we're bigger than the service, we're outside of the will of God. We go to church to praise the Lord. We do what we do in the sanctuary in service of the Lord. So if you're singing your song for congregational praise, you're singing the wrong song. If you're praying that prayer for a pat on the back from the Pastor, you're praying the wrong prayer.

Those of us that are bench members aren't beyond blame either. If you're coming to church *just* to hear the choir sing, you're missing out on what God has for you. If the devil rode shotgun with you on the way to church this morning, you're out of place. If you're having a personal problem with someone, the middle of service is not the time to act it out. Neither is Bible class. Neither is choir rehearsal. Neither is usher board meeting. Now, understand what I'm saying. If you've got a problem, take it to the Lord in prayer. Bring it to the altar on Sunday morning and leave it there. But the Bible clearly states that if you have a problem with your brother, you should go to him and him alone, and not the middle of the sanctuary.

This week, find out what your role is on God's program and play your part to His glory. Spend less time wondering whether or not the devil came to church on Sunday with someone else and spend more time making sure he didn't arrive with you. Is he in your heart? Is he in your mind? Is he in your attitude? We all have the capability of coming to church the wrong way. Like it or not, it's not always the other members of the congregation. If you read my work regularly, you know that I'm big on self evaluation. If we can't see the wrong in ourselves, if we can't see the wrong in our own families, if we can't see the wrong in our own friends, then we're likely to continue doing wrong. Remember, God's program is going on with or without you. If you haven't gotten with the program, either change or move on.

Week of April 25, 2010

Have you corrupted the village?

²Then make me truly happy by agreeing wholeheartedly with each other, loving one another, and working together with one mind and purpose. ³Don't be selfish; don't try to impress others. Be humble, thinking of others as better than yourselves. ⁴Don't look out only for your own interests, but take an interest in others, too – Philippians 2:2-4 (New Living Translation)

This week's email will be a little different, so bear with me please. As I was watching the news last week, I saw the story of a 14 year old girl found working at a strip club by her mother. The girl's mother says that she's mentally impaired. She says that she had no idea what her daughter was doing because the teen would sneak out at night after her and her husband went to sleep.

As for the strip club, they say the teen had a fake ID, she looks as old as that ID says she is and that this is all a misunderstanding and they shouldn't be held accountable. The strip club's so called "house mother" went as far as to blame this all on the girl's mother, saying that while she agrees that a strip club is no place for a teenager, if mom was on her job, this wouldn't have happened.

Now, I could tell a million stories that end up the same way as that one, but this is a weekly email, not a book. Unfortunately, a story like this truly is our new society in a nutshell. No one feels responsible for anyone else these days. No one cares about anyone else anymore. But there used to be a time when we protected one another. Were we perfect in the past? No, but there was a time when if a person wasn't living right, they didn't have the desire to take the world to hell with them. For example, if they weren't gonna lead you to the church, they'd take no part in you going to hell either. If they weren't gonna lead you to school, they wanted no part in you being a failure. If they saw that you didn't belong in a certain place, they'd send you away for your own good. Their misery was their own.

What this story and others like it says to me is that our communities have accepted what has become a trend these days. We're more willing to lead others astray than we are to point them in wise directions. In this instance, while it can be said that mom should've been a more diligent parent, the "I don't care" stance that the club employees took was what disturbed me more. Our communities (and whether you like it or not, if you have a strip club near you, it's part of your community) used to support one another. The point being, corruption of adults that make adult choices is one thing, but we should all be willing to protect our children from things such as this.

Unfortunately, we are operating under a different set of rules now. We don't seem to care if our neighborhoods burn down, our children underachieve and our moral fiber erodes. As long as we get ours, nothing else seems to matter. When our world was a better place to live in, it was because we genuinely cared for one another's well being. If a child in our circle was lost, we all felt it. If our neighbor was losing their home, we not only felt it with them, we may have even tried to help with some sort of fund raiser. Even though we weren't all spiritually sound, we were at least morally sound. No so much anymore.

This week, try and live outside of yourself. What that means is, we have to develop an attitude that suggests that what happens to someone else does matter to us. As a society, we can't continue to look the other way when a young man in the neighborhood or in the church seems off track. He's not just his parent's problem. If he decides to break the law on a regular basis, he becomes everyone's problem. We can't ignore our little girls when they're in need of guidance because if you're not careful, she becomes your daughter's best friend and a major influence on the decisions she makes.

We have to have a better understanding of the impact that we can have on our society. If we raise better children, we have a better world to look forward to. It still takes the entire village to do it. But as I wrote in *Temporarily Disconnected*, the villages are still raising our children. The problem is the villages are corrupt. If you've been receiving this email for some time, you've read my words as I declared that no child can really get off track without an adult's involvement. Because I've witnessed this firsthand with my own child, I know what I'm talking about. But what we need to recognize in the midst of this is that we're still influential when it comes to our children. We're influential in the schools, in the church and in the streets. We say they're not listening to us, but we couldn't be more wrong. The question is what are we telling them?

Are you about the message or the messenger?

[15]Study to shew thyself approved unto God, a workman that needeth not to be ashamed, rightly dividing the word of truth – 2 Timothy 2:15

What do you do when you wanna kill the messenger? We'll answer that shortly. Often when we enter our place of worship, we run the risk of having our feelings hurt. At some point during the service, something may be said from the pulpit that hits too close to home. Sometimes, it's so serious, we find ourselves staying away from the services in an effort to protect ourselves, all the while losing sight of the fact that you can run from a lot of things in life, but God ain't one of them.

While we have a knack for pointing our anger in the wrong direction, you would think that something like this wouldn't happen as often in church. The pastor or minister is there to give you the message that God has given to them. While it can be difficult to hear at times, we should know from our own studies whether or not we're being told right or wrong. This leaves me to wonder, why are we so hard on God's messengers?

Now, I understand that some of the places from which these messages flow aren't always the best. But I ask, if a pathological liar tells you that the sky is blue, is it not blue? Of course it is. In this instance, you wouldn't consider the source, you would consider the facts. Because you've done your "research", you know that the sky is blue no matter who's giving you the information. Why can't we do this in church?

We're struggling with God's Word because the culture in the church has changed. The culture in the church has changed because we have changed. Society has changed. But just because we have changed, doesn't mean that God or His Word has. Simply put, He's the same yesterday, today and forever, even if you aren't. So we must understand that while some of the traditions and ways of the church are different these days, the Bible that we have as a roadmap in life still needs to be adhered to.

Among other things, this is why our children struggle with God's laws. We as adults and leaders spend so much time refuting what's being said or going against our pastors when they say or do something we don't agree with, that our children don't know what and what not to adhere to. So we bring another societal issue into church. The issue of no one being able to correct our children. Neither the pastor, the deacons, the elders of the church, the mothers or anyone can correct our children in the ways of God's law, even if we can all see that they're wrong. There is a time to commit to your children, and that time is long before they make life mistakes.

We have to better educate ourselves on what God would have us to do and how we're supposed to live. If we don't educate ourselves, life will. We can't be angry at the message the pastors gives us. It's not their message. It's God's message. It's not the fault of the pastor that God wants us to live our lives according to His law. The pastor has to live under those same laws. We can't be angry at the laws or the covenants that the church upholds. These are God's laws. If you have a problem with what the Lord says, take it up with Him the next time you pray. That is, if you can find the time in between asking for blessings.

This week, study and show thyself approved. I don't know about you, but I get a little frustrated sitting in the service, watching the eyes roll every time the pastor says something that someone doesn't agree with. My aggravation is increased when the pastor is actually speaking based on the Word of God, and some that aren't educated in the Word seem annoyed.

The best way to find out if your pastor or someone in the church is leading you in wise directions is not to seek the court of public opinion. The best way is to study and know the Word yourself. This will keep us from developing attitudes when we're being told the rights and wrongs in relation to what God would have us do. You will know it for yourself. And when the opportunity presents itself, don't kill the messenger. Examine the message and see if it applies to you. If it does, examine yourself and see if a change is in order.

Week of July 18, 2010

"…known by your works…"

¹¹The lofty looks of man shall be humbled, and the haughtiness of men shall be bowed down, and the Lord alone shall be exalted in that day. ¹²For the day of the Lord of hosts shall be upon every one that is proud and lofty, and upon every one that is lifted up; and he shall be brought low
– Isaiah 2:11-12

Each week, I sit at this computer and I try to bring encouragement to everyone on my mailing list and those that they forward this message to. Now, a lot of you I've never met, but some of you I see on a regular basis. Either way, with these words that I write to you, I've created an expectation. I created an atmosphere like that of a minister. I've set myself apart on some level. Because of what I put out each week, people expect a certain behavior from me. But when you set yourself apart from people, you can go a couple of different ways. You can either exalt yourself or humble yourself. I pray to God that I stay in the latter.

As I continue to travel on my journey, I often tell my fiancée how important our relationship is. It's not only important because I feel that God has sent her to me, but it's important for the work that I'm trying to do. I tell her often that it is of great importance that I marry her because I am a role model. People are watching me to see if my words are matching up with my works. I've written in several books and pieces that I'd marry if God sent me a wife. He's done His part, so now I must do mine.

Whether you're doing this parent to child, teacher to student or most importantly, pastor to congregation, the moment you become a "do as I say, not as I do" person, you lose credibility and you lose people. The moment you become above the law, you abolish the law with your actions. No matter how beautiful or inspirational the words, how great the Bible class or how awesome the sermon, at some point, we are all measured. Not judged, but measured. This is just what happens. You will be measured to see if your works match your words.

It doesn't matter if I'm a writer, teacher, minister or whatever, if I'm delivering God's message, I can never become bigger than that message. I can never become bigger than the mission. I can never separate myself from the laws that God expects all of us to govern ourselves by. The moment I do that, not only do I lose with anyone reading these words, I lose with God. What I write each week is for all of us, and that includes me. Some of you have emailed me often to say that you need this weekly, but I'm telling you I need it, too.

There's no way that I can be charged with delivering information to God's people and not be expected by God to live by that same information. God has not appointed me to be a dictator. God has appointed me to be a messenger. When my message comes from God, it isn't simply a message that says "Go and tell these people how I want them to live". The message says "This is how I want you to live. Now, go and spread this message to others so that they too might live this way".

As Christians, our example and role model is Jesus. He was the Word in the flesh. He was sent here with a mission. The point here is if Jesus wouldn't stray from the mission, how can I? If a man that was sent here to be crucified for sins he never committed can follow through on what God has ordered, how can I not follow through on God's commandments? How can I be charged with leading God's people in any way and fall short because I feel as though I've reached a level of supreme knowledge and the laws don't apply to me anymore?

This week, I want you to remember something that I say regularly to my Bible class now: You are known by your works, not your words. If they don't match up, you've got a problem. This isn't a call to perfection because everyone knows that we aren't. But if the people that are listening to you can't see that you're trying to live as you speak, you've got a problem. Furthermore, if the people that are listening to you see that you appear to be above the laws that you expect them to be governed by, then, as the old folks used to say, you will catch hell. And if you don't practice what you preach, half your congregation walks away and the other half simply goes deaf on you.

Is it the way of The Lord?

⁷When a man's ways please the Lord, He maketh even his enemies to be at peace with him – Proverbs 16:7

Have you ever seen one of those action movies? The ones with one of those renegade cops that lives by his own rules and no one can tell him what to do? The force would love to get rid of him, but they can't because he gets the job done. At some point during the movie, he may get into a car chase with the bad guy. This criminal is bringing terror to the city, so somebody's gotta take him down. However, during that car chase, he crashes other cars, tears up a few buildings and shoots recklessly in the streets. He tears up the city and causes millions of dollars in property damage, all to catch one guy. Sure, it's entertaining because it's a movie. But if this were real life, it would hardly seem worth it. But, hey, it's just a movie, right?

That scenario sounds like us. At times, we will destroy everything in our path to get what we want. It takes someone watching our "movie" to ask us, is it really worth all of this? At that point, we stop and remind them, it's just a movie. Or better yet, it's my life. But we do want them to stay until the end of the movie, right? I mean, when most of us find happiness, we wanna share it with those closest to us. We want them to be happy with us and for us.

However, this doesn't always happen. It's not always possible. Sometimes, our happiness begins to affect others in a negative way. The first inclination is to assume that all of these people are just bitter or jealous of what we have. Our egos will always make us feel that everyone else wants to be us. But is that really the case when someone is not on board with what we're doing? Should we automatically assume that anyone not in agreement with us is a threat to our happiness?

One of the most dangerous mindsets to have is one that suggests that you live in this world by yourself. Like that opening scenario, you may catch the bad guy, but you destroyed my neighborhood to do it. What this means is we can't assume that what we do affects us and only us. We've talked about this before, but it bears repeating. When your "happiness" is separating you from family, friends and those that care for you, you have to re-evaluate what it is that you're doing. Simply put, God is about bringing us together, not tearing us apart.

When we find ourselves outside of God's will, but in a place that we wanna be in, we often try and explain away our behavior. But, understand this, when something has been ordained by God, it needs no validation. It needs no repeated explanation. It needs no affirmation. All of these things are already done if what we've done has truly been ordained by God. And believe it or not, other Christians can already tell. They don't need to be convinced. When what we're doing pleases God, that last thing we should worry about is opposition.

God will put us in situations to succeed if we allow Him to. However, we can't be naïve and think that God will stop us from making all mistakes. We have free will, so we can make our own decisions. We have the responsibility of choosing right from wrong. We can't be of the mindset that God will correct all of our situations, so we can do whatever we want. God will change your situation at times. He will improve certain situations at times. But if you're in a wrong situation, you're just wrong and you need to remove yourself from that situation. While God gives us unconditional love, He doesn't give the "unconditional support" that we always want in order to validate our wrongdoing. The conditions for His support are in His Word.

This week, think about what it's costing you. It's easy to become fixed on what we want and forget about everything else in life. But we must remember that God has no desire for us to be selfish in our wants. We as Christians are supposed to take joy in each other's happiness. We're supposed to share each other's happiness. Sometimes, we end up in wrong situations because we've ignored what God has told us. We can't continue thinking that God makes right out of wrong.

It is God that determines what is right and wrong, so in order to change wrong to right, He'd have to change His mind. That's not the way this goes. If we're wrong, we have the responsibility to get right. We have to look beyond what we're chasing sometimes and consider what the pursuit is causing. If my happiness causes misery to those closest to me, there may be something wrong with my choice. It's true that we can't spend all of our days trying to please everyone. But if the choices you're making in life are only designed to please you, those choices may require more thought.

Do you have the knowledge?

¹Brethren, my heart's desire and prayer to God for Israel is, that they might be saved. ²For I bear them record that they have a zeal for God, but not according to knowledge. – Romans 10:1-2

Looking at our society today, we seem to be overrun with criminal activity. As the years go by, the crimes seem to get worse and worse. While we look to find answers to this problem, we usually come to the conclusion that if we raised better children, we'd live in a better world. While that's certainly true, there's one element we can't ever underestimate: Education.

I'm a firm believer that when people are educated, they do better. It's not 100 percent, but it does matter. You get an education and that leads to a better job, better money and a better life. All things of value. All things that you wouldn't want to lose by committing a crime. So, you think before you act because you understand actions and consequences. You understand that you have options.

Not only can education keep you free from a physical jail, it can keep you free from a spiritual jail as well. We don't study the Word as much as we should and it leads to other poor decisions that we make in life. Some of us can't live as God wants us to because we simply aren't studying enough to know how. While we're all caught up in who is and who isn't living right, only a few of us can point to specifics in The Word to support why we feel the way that we feel.

You can go to just about any church on Sunday morning and you'd hear a pastor imploring his people to come to Bible class. While he's doing that, if you went through the minds of each member, you'd find a million and one excuses of why people can't make it out. I know that because it used to be me. Something that's good for you and free, and we can't even give it away. But let us offer something across the pulpit that's not as good for you and will actually cost you something, and we'll line up with our money.

What always struck me as odd is that you can get more people in a church for a concert or a play than you can for a Bible class. Not that any of that is bad for you if it's being done to the glory of God, but follow my point. More people will come to church to hear their favorite song being sung by the choir than to hear the message. More people are more aware of whether or not they've been slighted by someone in the church than they are of what the pastor spoke about or what the Word says we should do when someone is treating us wrong.

The reality is we are able to commit, we just need to remember what to commit to. Your commitment to God and His Word must be stronger than any other commitment that you have. More than your boyfriend or girlfriend, more than your "position" in the church, more than any Saturday night ballroom hustle or any Sunday morning gospel song. Even more than the church itself. We must return to a place where we understand that nothing takes the place of the Word. We shouldn't take it for granted, we shouldn't postpone it and we shouldn't omit it. It is the basis of all that we do in the church. How can we claim to follow that which we know nothing about?

Some of us can't do better as Christians because we don't know any better. We don't educate ourselves in the way of the Lord. And just like the criminals of the world, if we don't know better, we won't do better. Just like the criminals, if we don't learn to make better choices, the consequences can be dire. What I've tried to do with my work is point a person to God's Word so that they may know for themselves how He wants them to live. It's not that we don't love the Lord. We just need to develop that love based on knowledge and not routine or habit.

I understand that reading the verse at the top of my email is the only time that some people will read the Word of God each week. However, it is my desire that what I do here will encourage people to study more. If not for themselves, then just to see if I know what I'm talking about. We often have a desire to dispute man, but there's no disputing God. This is why we're quick to challenge God's preacher when he says something we don't like. We're picking a fight that we feel we can win rather than going to the source.

This week, make time to learn about what God would have you to do. We have a habit of getting so caught up in "living", that we forget to acknowledge the giver of life. We get so caught up in our jobs that we forget to bring a study of the One that gave us the job into our routine. We give God a little time on Sunday morning, sometimes reluctantly, and we act as though we don't have enough energy to give Him anything else. I thank Him regularly that He doesn't operate with us the way we do with Him.

Are you resisting the call?

¹⁰Create in me a clean heart, O God; And renew a right spirit within me ¹¹Cast me not away from thy presence; And take not thy Holy Spirit from me ¹²Restore unto me the joy of thy salvation; And uphold me with thy free spirit ¹³Then will I teach transgressors thy ways; And sinners shall be converted unto thee – Psalm 51:10-13

I've been busy over the last month trying to show others the importance of leadership. In the midst of doing so, I've found that some people are resistant to the idea. As it is with so many things that we're called to do as Christians, we fail to see the benefits that come with doing what God would have us do.

What's interesting to me is the fact that what's being said in the verses that I've chosen for this week message sounds a lot like what we do on a regular basis. "Lord, give me this, and I'll do that for You". However, once the Lord does "this", we find all the reasons in the world not to do "that". Why is that? Maybe we aren't as saved as we think we are.

There's a process we all must go through in order to truly be saved. It's not as simple as joining the church or reading the Word. We must become pure of heart. The Word says in Matthew 5:8 that by doing so, we shall see God. That's some blessing, isn't it? However, we can't always appreciate that with our human eyes. We only know the blessings that we see. So it's easy for us to put the importance of seeing God out of our minds when all we can think about is what we want while we're here on earth.

In order to do God's work, we not only must be spiritual, we must have the <u>right</u> spirit. The truth is, we're all spiritual in one way or another. The question is, what kind of spirit are you coming with? Singing in church is one thing, but are you praising or are you performing? Shouting in church is one thing, but are you shouting because you're filled with the spirit or because God is trying to work another spirit out of you? The answer to that lies between you and the Father. And be honest because you can fool me, but you can't fool Him.

The challenge that we have before us is the challenge of become a new being in Christ. Something else this week's verses suggest is something that I'm always calling for each and every one of us to do often: self examination. We must first become new in Christ before we can even begin to show anyone else the way of God.

While there are those that resist the call of leadership, it seems to me that they are resisting the call to examine themselves. In order to lead, not only do I have to be that example for others, I must check myself regularly. I must align myself with His word. I must be honest with myself when I'm haven't. I must do all the things that the Psalm suggests in order for God to restore that joy within me. But once I receive those blessings from God, I can't be selfish with it. I must lead others to Christ.

This week, allow God to create that clean heart within you. Allow Him to restore that joy inside of you. You won't believe how blessed you can be by simply humbling yourself to Him. But it doesn't end there. You must go forward. God won't bless you just so you can keep it to yourself. You are required to become a blessing to someone else. You are required to lead someone else to Christ.

You must fulfill the entire prayer in that Psalm. Once God has given you that clean heart and given you joy, you must teach transgressors the way. You must do your part to convert sinners to His way. Otherwise, you're failing to fulfill your purpose. I don't know about you, but I wouldn't want to be the one to shortchange God.

February 18, 2009

"I thought you were a Christian…"

Okay, this one hit me last Sunday. I overheard this comment from a person that disagreed with the way another person handled a particular situation. Not "I disagree with you", not "I would've handled it different", not even "let's agree to disagree", something we all need to learn to say from time to time. No, we got to judgment quicker than Judge Judy. "I thought you were a Christian". Now, the person accused of not being a Christian has more Christianity in one hand than…well, I won't go there. Let's just say that it should never be questioned, even if the accused has done something that the accuser disagreed with. Maybe it's me, but it seemed to be a harsh thing to say to someone that you simply disagree with.

I've been accused of being too analytical at times, but I believe that it's served me well. And I broke this one down in my mind over and over again. To me, to say to someone, "I thought you were a Christian", suggests that you just found out that they're not. It's like saying, "I thought you were a Leo". I'd only say that if I just found out you were a Cancer or Virgo, right? Otherwise, it makes no sense to say it. It should never come out of your mouth unless you're suggesting on some level that this person that you're speaking to is in fact not a Christian. As the saying goes, who made us judge, jury and executioner?

Where do we get off questioning another's Christianity? If you disagree with how another is living, then that's your prerogative. If you disagree with how they may have gone about something, then that's fine too. And the reality is, there are many out there that claim to be Christian, but they exhibit some behavior that's far from that. At the same time, we'll sometimes catch someone at a bad moment and assume that they're that way all the time. But are your affairs so much in order that you're in a position to question their relationship with God?

This kind of "judgment" comes about sometimes when we come across a Christian that happens to be in a state of anger or frustration. The biggest misconception about those who happen to be Christian or spiritual is that we're all so meek. We never have problems, we never raise our voices, we never get angry and, of course, we never sin. Contrary to popular belief, although we may have turned our lives over to God, we're still human. We still come from planet earth. We're still subject to the same things that those that live a secular life are subject to. We've just realized that we can't make it alone. When we fall short, we know how to get right with God.

If you've ever really listened to the sermons in your particular church or ever really understood The Word, you'd notice that the messages are given in general terms. Because your Pastor has no idea who's really living right or who's living wrong. He's giving you a message that God has given to him. If it applies to your life, then use it. If not, simply take it as a cautionary tale.

While we're casting stones based on one moment when a person may seem to be on the wrong side of Christianity, out of sorts or just having a bad day, we mustn't forget the words of the Bible that we're thrusting in their face. Judge not, lest ye be judged. Let he who is without sin cast the first stone. Get your house in order. Need I go on? While it's difficult to do so, we should never question another's relationship with God simply because we may disagree with something they've said or done. We should never be so high and mighty that if someone doesn't think or act the way that we feel they should that we're ready to send them to hell. No matter what some of us think, we don't have a Heaven or a hell to put anyone into. If that were the case, we'd all send someone to either of those places that didn't necessarily deserve to be there, just because of how we feel about them.

The worst thing about this is sometimes, the people that are throwing out the accusations are throwing them at people that have more than exemplified a Christian's mentality.

These are people that have done the work of God and you can almost bet that they'll see the Kingdom. But I guess that's what makes someone question the Christianity in the first place. You're so used to seeing that Christian behavior and attitude that you're completely caught off guard when you see something different. However, if I've shown myself to be a Christian on more days than not, shouldn't my track record speak for itself? Short of cursing out everyone from pillar to post, shouldn't we allow one another to express human emotion? Am I really going to your hell after one bad day? If that's the case, I'd hate to serve that unforgiving god that you serve.

This isn't just a church thing either, it's a society thing. We love to point fingers and throw accusations around. But we all need to learn to be a little more patient with others and show a little more understanding. If you're questioning someone's Christianity, surely you've never exhibited the behavior you're taking this stand against, right? And if you're sitting back questioning someone's Christianity, then you must know a thing or two about God, right? If that is the case, then you should know about forgiveness. If you're questioning, then you must have witnessed something that caused you to do so. And while we all like to tell people where to go, it doesn't mean that they have to or will. Like it or not, we're not in charge.

This is the type of behavior that keeps the sinner from coming to church and turning their lives over to God. We as "Christians" will pass judgment on those in the congregation that actually have turned their lives over to God, simply because we have a disagreement. If I'm a person with real problems, that's in real danger of seeing the fires of hell, do I really feel that I'd be better off with all of the "Christians" that can't stop passing judgment on each other? Probably not.

The temptation to correct individual behavior is always high. But you should only do that with your children. Adults are responsible for themselves. Deep down inside, we all think we know what's best. I have a website, for God's sake. Granted, I write books, so I need to promote my work, but this isn't my first one. I had one years ago, long before blogs were popular, just so that I could voice my opinion. But there's a difference between telling a group of people they're not living right and telling an individual they're not living right. If you're telling a group, the individuals that you're speaking to have to search within themselves to find out whether what you're saying applies to them or not. It's completely up to them.

However, if you're speaking to an individual, there's not doubt about who you're speaking to and what you're saying about them. The trick is, you'd better have your stuff together, you'd better have facts to back up your statements, and most of all, you'd better be right. Otherwise, it could get ugly, just as the conversation that brought about this piece did. If you're a millionaire giving someone financial advice, this kind of thing makes sense because you obviously know what you're talking about. If you're a successful business owner giving someone advice about starting their own business, you obviously know what you're talking about. But when it comes to Christianity and questioning a person's relationship with God, we all need to learn to tread lightly. Salvation truly is a personal thing.

"To inspire those in need of inspiration..."

Week of April 5, 2009

Publishers of peace

[7]How beautiful upon the mountains are the feet of him who brings good news, who publishes peace, who brings good news of happiness, who publishes salvation, who says to Zion, "Your God reigns." – Isaiah 52:7

I was recently asked what the inspiration was for me starting the weekly email. While spirituality is important to me, I don't claim to be a preacher. I'm just a son that really, really believes in his Father. In fact, for all of those out there that choose to follow the devil and his marching orders, my Daddy can beat up your daddy any day of the week. Just name the time and place. I'm just sayin'.

While we all aren't called to preach, we are all responsible for spreading the good news. We see the preachers of the world and we talk about the calling that God has placed on their lives. What we fail to fully recognize sometimes is that God has placed a calling on all of our lives. We all have a responsibility to tell someone of the goodness of God, share a message of peace and to talk about being saved. While I've covered many different topics in my work, from race to politics to love to the black community, all of what I've done has been based in spirituality. While I look to inspire my people through my words, I always want to try and bring the goodness of God to the forefront of all that I do. How beautiful is that?

What this weeks verse speaks to is the fact that there's joy in spreading the goodness of God. We can take our words, our news, our music, our movies and whatever else we have and spread messages of hate, dysfunction, greed, destruction and anything else you can think of, and the world will just eat it up. But why not be a publisher of peace? Why not talk about salvation? Why not tell someone how much better life can be when you have God in it?

The world is watching us, whether we're on our best behavior or not. So we have to show a real difference between what goes on in the Christian world and what goes on in the secular world. Now, what we can't do is over analyze ourselves and try to come off as Super Christians. This is where we fall short. We need to learn to identify with our brothers and sisters that are out in the world simply because we do. If we aren't still doing some of the things that they do, we've been there before. But we know our way home. Why not show them the way?

This week, be a publisher of peace. Share your good news with someone. God has all kinds of blessing for us when we tell the world of His goodness. But don't let the blessings be your motivation. We should tell the world that God is good simply because He is. If you're reading this email right now, you are blessed, no matter what your current situation is.

My hope is that we will one day cease measuring the goodness of God in cars, money and houses. We fall short sometimes because when we're missing those kinds of blessings, we feel less than overjoyed and it shows to the outside world. But the God we serve is bigger than wars, bigger than hate, bigger than family dysfunction, bigger than addiction and bigger than anyone's messed up economy. I bring you good news, my brothers and sisters. Your God reigns!

Week of June 21, 2009

Wherever you go, take the Lord with you

[6] ... "Go in peace. The journey on which you go is under the eye of the LORD." – Judges 18:6

Life can be so nice. It's a wonderful world. A paradise. That's taken from a song I know. I'm willing to bet that only one of you on the email list knows where it came from. Maybe two. And don't go looking to Google it and emailing me back to try and fool me. I'll know if you try to trick me. But, I digress. This isn't about music trivia because if it were, I could write all day. There is truth in those lyrics. Life truly can be nice. Even in the midst of all that we face, it can be a wonderful world and even a paradise at times.

As we reach the summertime months, a lot of us will be traveling. Usually when we do our summer travel, we're going to places of enjoyment. We're vacationing with families or our significant others, enjoying a bit of that wonderful world that I mentioned in the last paragraph. We'll be in planes, trains and automobiles seeking to reach our destinations safely. We'll frantically pack our bags with both excitement and uncertainty. The excitement of travel and the uncertainty that comes with being sure that we've packed everything that we need and forgotten nothing.

Nothing is worse than being 500 miles away from home and realizing that you've forgotten something vital. Could you imagine the tears that would be threatening to roll down my face if I left for my family reunion this July, only to find out that I've forgotten my computer? The pain of having to be engaged the whole time. The pain of not being able to write down my perspective on what I've seen. The agony of not being able to send you this weekly email. Never fear, though. I'd forget a change of clothing before that happened. The work must continue.

However, when we do travel and we forget to pack this or that, it usually isn't as dire as I just made it seem. More times than not, we've forgotten something that we could easily go two or three days without. And in a worse case scenario, we can run to the store and replace it if it's that important. And trust me, if I left my computer, that email will still be forthcoming as long as I have my precious CrackBerry (BlackBerry for those unaware; it is addictive) by my side. But the bottom line is we've never left home without anything that would prevent us from reaching our destination. We may not make it with all of the things that we wanted to bring, but we still have the essentials to get where we were going.

As I have been on my own personal journey for peace in recent years, I have decided to pack light. Sometimes on those weekend getaways, we try to carry things on the journey that we really can do without. But we can't travel that way anymore if we really want peace. For me, there were some bad habits that I realized I couldn't travel with anymore. There were some ways that I couldn't travel with anymore. There were some relationships that I couldn't travel with anymore. There were even some friends and family that I couldn't travel with anymore. Although I haven't completely arrived yet, I came to realize that there were only a couple of essentials that I needed to travel with in order to reach my destination. Two things that can't be replaced with a quick trip to the store: God and His Word.

At the last few KJWorld Roundtables, we've been trying to define our purpose in life and trying to reach a level of peace within. Seemingly two separate journeys, but in reality, it is the same journey. Because once you know what that purpose is in life and line that purpose up with God, your life will become more peaceful. Now, this isn't to suggest that your life will be without trouble. It isn't to suggest that it will be without struggle. It is to suggest that once the definition of your life includes God, life can be so nice. It's a wonderful world. A paradise. When you know that God is with you, no journey seems too long. No destination seems too far. No peace seems unattainable. All you have to do is keep God and His Word with you no matter where you go and you're sure to be blessed.

⁵Trust in the LORD with all thine heart; and lean not unto thine own understanding. ⁶In all thy ways acknowledge Him, and He shall direct thy paths. – Proverbs 3:5-6 (Thanks Ma)

This week, this month, this summer and for this life, take no journey without God and His Word. Too often, we travel this earth and through this life with our eyes firmly fixed on our destination, but not in acknowledgement of The One that will get us there. While we know that God is everywhere, that's more of a statement of fact. That doesn't mean that we're always traveling with Him. That doesn't mean that we brought Him along for the journey. It's simply means that God is always wherever you are anyway. For some of us, that's not always a good thing because we're sometimes places where we shouldn't be. On second thought, maybe that *is* a good thing. Obey that voice, get out of that place and back on your journey. I don't know about you, but my bag only has the essentials. My God and my Bible. Okay, my computer and my CrackBerry are in there too, but you understand, right?

Week of June 28, 2009

Addressing the man in the mirror

¹Judge not, that ye be not judged ²For with what judgment ye judge, ye shall be judged: and with what measure ye mete, it shall be measured to you again – Matthew 7:1-2

Let's start this week off with a little poetry: When I look into the mirror, I only see me/But how comfortable am I with what I see? I'll let you guys have that one for free. While we all ponder that question, I can't help but wonder how many of us will be honest with our answers. We point fingers a lot in life, but where man has always struggled is in the area of self examination. Do we really feel that we're that much better than anyone else or are we simply afraid of what we'll find if we dig too deep within ourselves?

This week, something rare happened in the world. Someone that we all knew (although not personally) died. And while Michael Jackson's death sent shockwaves throughout this country and the world, he's just as polarizing in death as he was in life. Hours and hours will be spent dissecting who he was as a man and so on and so forth. And as it is with so much that happens in life, we spend more time speaking ill of one another than we do listening to one another. Way back in 1987, Michael urged all of us to do some self examination and look at the man in the mirror. And what did we do with the information? We sat back and questioned whether or not he took his own advice. Once again, we've missed the point.

I can't help but wonder if this is what happens when we come to service on Sunday morning. I'm not ashamed to say out loud that there are times in our Sunday morning service when I'm not sure why some people are there. I often ask the question in my head, "If you didn't come to praise Him, then why are you here?" Don't misunderstand me. We're no different than any church out there. The spirit moves in Zion Hill Baptist Church on Sunday mornings, especially when our young people are involved. But the devil comes to our church, too. Just like he comes to your church. Sometimes he comes alone and sometimes he piggybacks on us. All because we fail to do a self-check from time to time. All because we fail to look into that mirror and be honest about what we see.

In these emails and in my other work, I often speak of self correction. I firmly believe that true change comes from within. It doesn't come from other people telling us what's wrong with us and then we accept it and do something about it. All that others can do for us is make observations based on what they see outwardly. But it's up to each individual to look inwardly and decide if what's being said has merit. The only people that know what's really true about you are God and you. You can lie to me and if you're willing to, you can lie to yourself when that reflection is staring back at you in the mirror. But you can't lie to God.

How about some more poetry: So what do you do when the unflattering is true?/What do you do when God is trying to reach you? That may need to be written out one day. But, I digress. Are we missing the preacher's message because we'd rather judge his deeds? Are we not being fulfilled because we've fixed our eyes on a man's human qualities as opposed to listening to what he has to say? Is the fact that the man of God is still prone to mistakes keeping you from connecting with the message that God is delivering to you through him? While I understand that it's hard to take advice from someone that's flawed themselves, at what point in your lives have you not done this? Who amongst us has no flaws? Get your mirrors out people.

5A wise man will hear, and will increase learning; and a man of understanding shall attain unto wise counsels – Proverbs 1:5

While we all enjoy sitting back in judgment, we're never really as critical of ourselves as we are of others. I do believe that God delivers us messages in unlikely packages just to see if we're paying attention. That message could be from a child's mouth. That message could be from a homeless person on the street. That message could be from someone that you refuse to speak to anymore. Or it could be from someone as "strange" as Michael Jackson. The path to true wisdom is being able to learn from any person, any thing or any situation that you encounter in this life.

This week, we all need to continue to examine ourselves. And for those of you that feel that you do a good job of this already, we could all use a tune-up from time to time. Life isn't about what we do when we feel that we've arrived. Sometimes, it's about how much further you're willing to go. In my next book, I talk about the vanity of Christianity. We sometimes become so "filled with the Holy Spirit", that we forget that we will always be a work in progress. We will never be all that we should be in this life. But the only way to continue on with positive results is to be honest when we look into our personal mirrors. When the song "Man In The Mirror" implores you to "make that change", we shouldn't just shrug it off. No matter what you may have felt about the man singing it, it's literally sound advice.

Cleaning up your spiritual house

[11]The house of the wicked shall be overthrown; but the tabernacle of the upright shall flourish – Proverbs 14:11

Have you ever lost or misplaced something in your house and you couldn't find it to save your life? Isn't that a great feeling? Well, maybe not. You go from room to room to room frantically in search of that pair of scissors, those gloves, that shirt that matches the rest of that outfit, that one sock or the remote. And when do we go looking for these things? At the very moment that we need them the most. Otherwise, you wouldn't be looking for it, right? And just when you've had it, just when you're as frustrated as you can be looking all over the place, just when you've used all of the most colorful language that you can to describe that missing whatever it is that you're looking for and you're about to give up, it reveals itself. Of course it was right there. That's where you left it. After all, it's always in the last place you look. Because to keep looking after that would make no sense, right?

A lot of us spend time rummaging through our spiritual lives like this. Searching for things that we feel are missing, but knowing it's around here somewhere. But in this case, it's not so much about misplacing as it is about our spiritual lives being cluttered. Sometimes we can't find what we're looking for because we have too much other junk lying around. While we're pretty good at "blaming" God for some of the things that go missing in our lives, we have to learn to take inventory of our own lives from time to time.

God has already blessed us in ways that we either don't realize or appreciate. All of the other things that we have are things that we've picked up along the way and filled our spiritual houses with. Some of us have good families, but we don't appreciate them as we should. Where we should be about togetherness, we have a spirit that insists on division and disharmony. We still haven't figured out that there's strength in that togetherness, but when we begin to separate from one another in that spirit of division and disharmony, the devil is not only pleased, he thrives. It is his joy to see us at odds with one another.

God has also placed quality friends in our lives, and yet we take them for granted. I spoke about this in *Peace In My Mind*. Friends just aren't what they used to be. We sell each other out over just about nothing nowadays. While a good friend was always hard to find, it seems that even the ones that we thought we had are hard to hold on to. Loyalty seems non-existent these days.

This exists in our relationships as well. Having the right man or woman in your life is only a good thing if you appreciate what you have. It doesn't mean a thing if you don't take care of your relationship. It doesn't mean a thing if you refuse to appreciate what God has placed in front of you until it's gone. You can't expect a person to wait for you forever. Let's be real. If they're that good, you aren't the only one that noticed. There's probably a line for that. If you get your shot and you blow it, you can't blame them and you certainly can't blame God. If you're the only one in the mix that didn't do their part, look in the mirror, own up to it and have a seat until the next bus comes along.

What we must remember as Christians is that all is never lost. Our God is still alive! Sometimes, we just need to clean up that spiritual house a bit and get rid of some of the clutter because, as this week's verse suggests, the house of the upright will be blessed. That better relationship with your spouse or significant other is in the house. And yes, it is in the last place you left it. It's lying underneath the lies and infidelity that the two of you have brought home. That better relationship with your parents is there. It's over behind that spirit of disobedience, disrespect and disregard for the Fifth Commandment that you brought home last month. That better relationship with your family is there. The problem is, you put it in the same bag with that dysfunction and disharmony that you like to bring whenever you come to the house for family get-togethers. Even that better relationship with your Pastor is in the house. You took it off the mantle when you and the devil decided that causing trouble in the church looked better up there.

This week, I want you all to take a look around your spiritual house. Take a good look around. What do you see? After doing that, ask yourself 3 questions:

1. How have I lived?
2. How am I living
3. How will I live from this day forward?

While some of the things that bring disharmony to our lives are beyond our control, some of them are our own doing. We lie on one another, and we expect to find peace. We steal from one another and we expect to get somewhere in life. We disrespect one another and yet we pretend to be so wrapped up in The Word. We don't love each other as we should and yet we claim to be on our way to Heaven. Some of us are so bad that not only is our house a mess, we'll come and tear up someone else's house before cleaning our own. But if we can't answer questions 2 and 3 in a positive manner, then I have a 4th question for you: How much has to go wrong in our lives before we understand the message that God is trying to send us?

Week of September 13, 2009

Be inspired so that you may inspire

[35]Then Jesus said unto them, "Yet a little while is the light with you. Walk while ye have the light, lest darkness come upon you; for he that walketh in darkness knoweth not whither he goeth. [36]While ye have light, believe in the light, that ye may be the children of light… - John 12:35-36

As I've taken this weekly journey since February, I've received lots and lots of feedback on my messages. Most of you tell me to keep up the good work, and I appreciate that. But there are two forms of gratitude that I enjoy more than others. First, I appreciate it when I'm told that my message hit home and it was what was needed in someone's life. After all, that's one of the main reasons I do this. I want to strike a chord in someone. Through what's on my mind or through my personal experiences, I hope to help those reading my emails to improve upon themselves as I try to do the same. At the end of the day, I believe we're all on the same journey.

However, there's one thing that I love to hear more than anything. I love to hear that my message has actually inspired someone. This is how I want to be thought of. An inspiration. I don't need fame and I don't need fortune. To inspire my people in a positive way through my work would be my reward. While there are forms of good and bad inspiration, the good is more readily acknowledged. We can inspire people to do just about anything, but when we inspire them to do good things with their lives, we can in turn define our own legacy. We're not always mindful of this, but maybe it's time we change that. By inspiring others in a positive way, we can become more appreciated for how we're trying to live. This is what I want for my work. This is what I want for myself.

What I've come to realize is that we revere people of a certain level of fame and wealth because of what they have, but not so much for what they do for others. Even when they actually do good things for others, we bury it in the back of our minds and focus more on what they have, what they're wearing or who they're sleeping with. I believe that this is what drives us to seek these things at times in our lives. We want the attention that comes with those things. But everyday people like you and me are remembered more for what we do. We're remembered more for how we live. We're remembered more for what we will or won't give. We don't always like that, but it's the truth. If you're aware of this fact, then it usually changes the way that you live. When you're aware of this fact, you're more aware of what you give back.

It's often said that the best things in life are free, and I believe that wholeheartedly. When people read some of my emails, some of them will remind me that people are getting paid for what I'm dishing out for free through email. And while I understand that, I also understand that we can't always look to gain financially for helping someone spiritually. We can't always look to gain financially for sharing our God-given gifts. We have to learn to give because we're blessed and able and not for profit or other gain. Besides, I refuse to place my limitations on God. I have no doubt that He can give me enough knowledge to fill up my books and give you a weekly email. It is my pleasure to share with you what He gives to me. If I can be someone's light in darkness, I have been blessed. And if I ever inspire any of you to live better, then I'm already paid in full.

This week, I'd like to challenge you to do two things. First, find your positive inspiration in life. Whatever that may be, if you haven't already found it, start seeking it right now. Start with God and you're almost there. But while God is the ultimate inspiration, we do need earthly inspiration as well. Second, once you've found that positive inspiration, share it with others so that they may be inspired as well. Remember that you have greatness within you and others can be inspired by that. Remember that others can be inspired by witnessing the joy we get from living as we're inspired to, just as they can be inspired to seek God by seeing God in us. It doesn't mean that they have to go out and do exactly as you do, but just by watching you live out your dream, someone can be inspired to chase theirs with a little more effort. They can be inspired to chase theirs with the same intensity that you're living yours with. Do this now while you still have the opportunity. We have a lot of living to do, but just a short time to do it. Just by showing others how God has blessed you, you can be inspiring.

Salvation is free

[26]For what is a man profited, if he shall gain the whole world and lose his soul? Or what shall a man give in exchange for his soul? – Matthew 16:26

Have you ever felt invincible? Maybe you got the right job, the right car, the best friends, the right man or woman in your life or you've got the right amount of decimals in your bank account. Sounds like a great feeling, doesn't it? Sitting on top of the world and no one can stop you. The only problem with being on top of anything is the fact that there's always someone or something looking to take you down. So when there's a crack in your super armor or when you come crashing to earth, it tends to be painful. But only if your priorities are not in order.

There has never been a truer statement than the fact that the best things in life are free. I'm sure that sounds familiar, but how many of us can really live by that? Turn on your TV once a day and I promise you that you'll see plenty of people with money and seemingly all that they could wish for, except real happiness. We once again witnessed a class meltdown by hip hop artist Kanye West on an awards show when he took the stage and stole a moment of joy from another artist. While I'm sure that ego, arrogance and alcohol fueled Kanye's act, there was also sadness and unhappiness there. I don't believe that he's ever properly grieved over losing his mother and for all of his millions, he's unhappy. Only someone that's unhappy can continuously try to make others unhappy with their actions as Kanye has.

Another example: During this week, I had the chance to watch the two day interview that Oprah did with fallen and now rising again star, Whitney Houston. At one point during the interview, the discussion turned to Whitney's drug abuse. At one point, she stated that the actual drugs weren't the entire problem, but that she was addicted to her ex-husband, Bobby Brown. So, as he went, so did she.

While some scoffed at this, I can see the reality of it. Sometimes, it really is about the company you keep. And this email isn't even long enough to get into Michael Jackson. While we've all watched these particular dramas unfold in front of our eyes over the years, we all tend to be shocked anytime a person of wealth struggles with life. Because we're just as guilty as they are of believing that their money will heal all of their wounds. But make no mistake about it, whether you're rich or poor, this world has more misery for you than joy. It makes you wonder why we're so intent on conquering something so sinful as opposed to changing it.

As a child, I wanted what a lot of children want. I wanted to be rich and famous. We didn't have much when I grew up, even though I didn't realize that until I was in my teens. But it made me crave for a better life. I'm sure that many people, both the rich and famous and otherwise, could identify with what I just said. Often, growing up poor can fuel you to great financial success.

However, there's a flip side to that. As I got older, I came to see a different perspective. As I got older, I clung more to what my mother gave me. That sense of pride in who I am no matter what I own. That sense that education was the most important thing that I could amass here on earth because if I'm educated and I use that education wisely, I will always be able to take care of myself. And most importantly, she gave me a spiritual center that's been the major difference in my life. If I keep God in my life, He will supply all of my needs, whether material or otherwise.

I also came to realize that I didn't necessarily have to use the fact that we didn't have much growing up as fuel to be rich. I could use it as an understanding that I don't need all the money in the world just to be happy. Because my mother made me happy by never letting us go hungry and never letting us do without any of the necessities. She was so good at what she did that I never knew how little we had until I was older and I looked back on my childhood. That's how I know how blessed I truly am to have the mother that I have. And God gave her to me for free.

This week, find out what truly makes you happy and live in pursuit of that. Now, for some of us, there's no getting around it. You like to spend and that's just how it goes. If that's you, then live it up. If that's where your happiness lies, then do you. But be sure to count up all the costs. Have you lost more than money? Have you alienated family and friends with your pursuits? Have you put yourself in jeopardy with your desire for the material things of this world? Have you put your soul in jeopardy in an attempt to gain this world, all of its riches and all of its ills? Give it some thought before you answer. But remember, while some of the best things in life and the best times that we'll have will sometimes cost us money, happiness is free. Love is free. Salvation is free.

Week of September 27, 2009

Embracing your evolution

[1]To every thing there is a season, and a time to every purpose under heaven: [2]A time to be born, and a time to die; a time to plant, and a time to pluck up that which is planted; [3]A time to kill, and a time to heal; a time to break down, and a time to build up – Ecclesiastes 3:1-3

If you live here in Michigan, you know what time of year it is now. Summer is fading away and we're moving into fall. For me, that's great news because that means football season. But for those of you that enjoy warm weather, that isn't good news because you know what comes with that fall weather. Colder temps and then on to winter. Then again, the holiday season comes with winter, so that's a good thing, right? So whether you like the changing weather and the cold temperatures or not, it seems that some good is still found in being a little uncomfortable for a while, right? Okay, maybe some of you could care less about football and some of you may not be into the holidays, but I think you get my drift.

What the changing seasons represent to me is evolution. It represents constant change. Now, this isn't change in a negative sense, as some of you have jumped ahead to late December/early January in your minds and you can just see 5 or 6 inches of snow on the ground. It's the nature of things. It's something necessary to get us to the next phase. I think that's why I'll always want to live in a place where I can experience all four seasons. Sure, being comfortable and staying in one place all the time might be what others prefer, but where's the fun in that? There's something about us humans that never wants to be uncomfortable. Even when we can sometimes see the benefits on the other side, we still want all of the fruits without planting any seeds. We want things to consistently go as we've planned.

However, our lives are quite similar to the changing seasons that we see. As fall and winter approaches, things tend to die off, just as it is sometimes in our lives. The cold weather takes away some things that have grown throughout the year. Maybe a bad habit dies off, maybe some unflattering behavior dies off, maybe a friendship dies off or maybe our love of the world dies off. When this happens, we often find ourselves huddled up in the house alone as we tend to do on a cool fall night or a cold winter's afternoon. But as I've stated so often in my work, being alone doesn't mean being lonely, and sometimes it's not only okay to be by yourself for a while, sometimes it's necessary.

But just as winter and fall can take some things away, when spring comes around, it's time for some brand new things to grow in our lives. That brand new feeling will be alive again in you. You just have to get through your fall and your winter in order to see those flowers bloom in your life. We have to understand that just as the changing weather is necessary, so is change in our lives. I don't know if I could properly appreciate spring if it weren't for winter. And while it'd be nice if I never had a day of trouble, those days help me appreciate the good times even more.

At the same time, we need to be understanding when other people change. We all have the right to be comfortable in who we are. Friendships sometimes fall apart because we can't accept the fact that someone is moving in another direction. While it's important to grow together when you're in a relationship, friendships are different. There's more room for individuality there. This is why it's so important to have a relationship with God. So that we can grow within it. So that we can become closer to Him. So that we can see all that He has to offer us.

This week, embrace your evolution. Understand that if you ain't changing, you ain't tryin'. While there can be consistency in your behavior, your morals and your values, you as an individual should always be striving for change. You should always be looking to get better. Seasons change and so should we. As we've talked about often in these emails, this can require your earthly self to walk alone from time to time, but as long as you're walking with God, you're never alone in spirit. Never fear the changing of the seasons in your life. When it gets cool, grab a jacket. When it snows, grab a shovel. And when spring comes back around, you'll appreciate that new beginning a little more.

Week of November 22, 2009

Perception can be reality in life

[16]Let your light so shine before men, that they may see your good works, and glorify your Father which is in Heaven – Matthew 5:16

A lot of us, myself included, will sometimes have the attitude that we could care less what people say or think of us. And while that may provide some peace of mind and maybe even a little bit of confidence for some, is it really how we're supposed to live? I know that in some instances, we're dealing with people that are looking to hurt us or bring us down by what they think or feel about us. In cases such as this, it's probably best to tune a deaf ear to what's being said. If a person doesn't care for you, then they're more likely to be unnecessarily critical of you. They're more likely to have a less than favorable opinion of you with no real basis for feeling that way. This is especially true when you have some sort of spirituality about yourself. When you seek to walk a different path in your life, those that still walk the way of the world will have something to say about that.

However, if you stop and think about it, how many people like that are a part of our circle of life? Oh sure, we all have our "haters" out there, some of us more than others. But are these the people that are most important to you in your life? I sincerely doubt it. Who looks to spend all of their time around people that they already know can't stand them? If that's you, maybe some therapy is in order. Outside of work associates and people that merely pass through our lives, our family and friends are the ones that truly define our lives.

I attended a funeral yesterday of a friend of mine. Actually, she was more than a friend. She was the first real girlfriend I ever had as a teenager. I've known her most of my life. We drifted apart as adults and her life was filled with ups and downs, but she was remembered quite fondly yesterday. While plenty of nice things are said about the deceased at homegoing services, having known who she was deep down inside, nobody lied yesterday. She was genuinely a good person. What I remember most about her was that if she cared for you, it was real and it never went away. I saw firsthand at the services yesterday that she was that way with everyone. As I looked around the church and saw that crowd of people that came to say goodbye, I realized that it mattered what they thought of her. Because if no one cared or thought anything of her, no one would've been there.

If you don't care what people say or think about you, that's fine and it certainly is your prerogative. But what that also means is that you can't be angry when others take a less than pleasant view of you. You can't be upset by the perceived reality of who you are. You can't be upset because someone forms an opinion of you based on how you dress, the language you use or the way you behave yourself in public if all those things are thought to be unbecoming. If it's what makes you comfortable, then by all means, do what you do. But you should also be prepared for the fallout.

Having this attitude can affect many of the relationships you have, personally, professionally, spiritually and otherwise. If you can handle that, then it's on you. But be sure that you're sure before you allow certain behaviors to close doors that you need open, and open doors to some situations that you never wanted to see in your life. It's understandable to not want anyone hating on you for your choices, but at the same time, you can't hate on them for disagreeing with them. Sometimes, perception is reality, whether fair or unfair, because it's all in the eye of the beholder.

This week, think about how the world sees you. Understand that everyday, you write your own history. If you lead a Spirit led life, you're going to have your detractors. You're going to have people that don't like you. You'll have people that unfairly judge you. But you must remember a few things before you go running around telling folks that it doesn't matter what they think about you. First, before you dismiss what they're saying, be sure to check yourself. Be sure that the negative perception of you isn't true. It's easy to dismiss the unflattering when it comes from a person that you don't get along with.

Second and most important, remember who you're living for. You're living for God. You're living for those people in your life that truly love and care for you. So it does matter what they think. There are people in your life right now that you should always consider before you act. There are people in your life whose opinions should matter to you. If this is not so, then we'll all live recklessly. Be that light that they can look to as an example of how to live. Be that light of encouragement to those that may be watching, because someone that's influenced by your words, your actions, your dress or the way you carry yourself is always watching. And while we sometimes only want to march to the beat of our own drum, we have to learn to be mindful of who's following along to our rhythm.

The spiritual green thumb

37Then saith He unto His disciples, "The harvest is truly plenteous, but the labourers are few;" 38 "Pray ye therefore the Lord of the harvest, that He will send forth labourers into His harvest" – Matthew 9:37-38

How's your garden? Didn't expect that question, did you? The way I see it, our lives are like gardens. This is what I think of when The Word tells us that we reap what we sew. As we go through life, we spend our days planting and harvesting. What you put into the soil of your soul is surely what will grow. I'm reminded of a passage from a poem I wrote called "Awake": "Our struggles in life will take to places/We're not sure we want to go/But all of the rain that falls in our lives/Causes flowers of character to grow". Indeed, trouble will come, but it's how you handle that trouble that defines you. It's what you've planted in the soil of your soul that will determine what grows when life rains a little drama in your life.

In the garden of my life, there are many things growing. It's not all perfect, but I'm doing my best to maintain. We're still doin' a little weeding over here. In years past, it wasn't always the best place to be fed. In the past, there were seeds of discord. They grew into a life filled with some sadness and uncertainty. Relationships failed and I didn't know why. Friendships that were no good for me we're plentiful. So whenever the harvest came, indeed, I had reaped what I had sewn. While my foundation was solid, it's all in what you do with what you know. It's all in how you use that foundation.

For example, if I'm spiritually built like a world class athlete but I eat nothing but junk food, how long will I be able to perform at an elite level? Sooner or later, my choices will catch up to me. Yes, there was plenty of misbehavior all throughout the garden. Unfortunately, the relationship I had with the dark side of myself was strong. When I took a long look at my garden, I realized why I wasn't being fed as I should've been. I realized why I was never full. I realized why I wasn't healthy. Part of living right is eating right. If the garden is poisoned, you will consume that poison. But all of that had to change. If was ever going to get better, I had to change the way I was doing things. I had to change my ways. Like my dear mother, I had to become a better gardener.

So when you find that your garden isn't bringing what you need it to bring, what do you do? That's when it's time to replant and replenish. That's when it's time to pull up the roots of all that's not bearing fruit in your life. That's when it's time to do a spiritual detox and rid yourself of all the unhealthy things that you've been ingesting all this time. That's when it's time to replace that with something more substantial. Something good for the soul. Something that will make you healthy. And believe it or not, you can plant things that will help you live forever. It's not an easy thing to do and that's why the "labourers are few", but your salvation depends on it. You must start by replanting the garden.

A few years ago, I replanted and replenished and I couldn't be happier. Uprooted were some old ways. Uprooted were some unproductive friendships. Uprooted were some negative thinking. What grew in it's a place? A better way of living. A better relationship with God. A better relationship with myself. More Sunshine than I could ever imagine. More happiness than I could've imagined. Yes, I have Peace In My Mind. Now, when I look out over my garden, I don't see the things that I used to see. I only see one thing growing: My breakthrough.

This week, go out and do a little gardening of your own. If you're finding things there that shouldn't be growing, then it's time to do a little uprooting. It's time to remove some of the weeds growing. It's time to make things a little more organic. Your soul is no different than your body. If you don't feed it things that can nourish and in turn help you to flourish, then it becomes unhealthy. It becomes lazy. It becomes at risk to all sorts of spiritual disease. And if it isn't taken care of, it could die on you. But we're greater than that, aren't we? We're better than that, aren't we? It's time to make use of your spiritual green thumb (some of you may have to look that one up). Don't worry about the rain that falls. Just make sure that your ground is fertile.

Week of December 27, 2009

The process of change

[17]Therefore, if any man be in Christ, he is a new creature: old things are passed away; behold, all things are become new – 2 Corinthians 5:17

As we come upon the end to another year, a lot of things tend to go through our minds. Most of us are still filled with a good feeling after Christmas and we still have lots of friends and family near. That good feeling that comes with the holiday season causes us to reflect and re-evaluate what's important in life. But more than anything, as we get closer to the New Year, there's usually one general thought: What have I done with the past 12 months and how can I do better with the next 12?

We often come into the New Year with great expectations. There's a level of excitement that comes with the newness of it all. And while it's great to be so inspired by one day of the year, it's sometimes hard to hold that focus all year 'round. What's so interesting about the New Year coming in is it's the one day that will cause you to look back and forward at the same time. You look back on the past year and think of all the things you did or didn't do, all the people you lost and found, all of your failures and successes and all of the things that you did one way, but will try and do differently come January 1st.

Too often, I've heard people say "I'll be glad when this year is over", as if life's drama works on a yearly basis. As though all the trouble that you're having is saying "We're running out of days! Let's give 'em hell over the net couple days because once 2010 hits, we can't cause problems anymore". If only the devil chose us that way. This type of mentality is superstitious in nature. It almost suggests that we need January 1st as some good luck charm or rabbit's foot of life. If we could just make it to the New Year, all of our problems will be solved. But if I have drama in my life at the end of October, what am I to do for the next two months while I wait for baby New Year to save me?

I think where we fall short is in making that conscience effort – or resolution for all of you that like to do that at 12:01am – to change ourselves not just for that moment, but for good. We can't always sit back and wait for the calendar to flip in order to change. I assure you that you're still the same person on 1/1 as you were on 12/31. Change doesn't happen in an instant. It's a process. It happens over time. If you make that resolution once per year and once per year only and you fall off by January 12th, then what are we to do with you? How should we deal with you reverting back to your old ways?

I support the idea of a brand new year and a brand new you. But something I'd like to see us do a little more is change when change is needed. Not just when someone calls us out, not when it benefits us and us only and certainly not just when the calendar flips. Do it when you see that it needs to be done. In fact, try a little preventative maintenance. If you see a problem developing, do something about it before it becomes an even bigger problem. If there are things in your life that need to change, they need to change now. If there are people in your life that need to be gone, they need to be gone now. If there are goals that you've set for the coming year, you should be working on them now. None of us are promised the New Year and that's why you never put off until tomorrow what you can do today.

Most importantly, what you must remember is how blessed you truly are. If you make it into the New Year, you have to realize that God is smiling on you. You may not be in the best physical or financial health, you may not have all of the things that your heart desires, you may not be as happy as you wanna be, but you're still here. There's still time. But we don't have forever, so we mustn't procrastinate. If you don't have joy, go out and get it. If you don't have peace, go out and find it. If your life is unfulfilled, do what is necessary to change that. We spend so much energy on things that make us miserable. Why not turn that energy around and make ourselves happy with it? Don't allow the 1st of January to hold you hostage. If you're carrying the burden of 2009 on your back, December 27th is just as good a day as any to lay it down. If you want change now, then have it right now.

This week, for the rest of this year and on into the next, remember that the best way to maintain that brand new you is to maintain that brand new you. In essence, don't place everything on one day of the year. Change when you recognize the need for change. Once you make that change, make a habit of re-evaluating and reassessing things as you go along. Not just for the year, but for your life. Sure, it's natural to measure things by year's end. As I said, the end of the year is about reflection on the past and looking to the future. But let's not put any undue pressure on ourselves to completely reinvent ourselves all in one day. Take your time. Do it piece by piece and step by step. You didn't become who you are in one day, so it stands to reason that it'll take more than a day to change it. Happy New Year and God bless you all.

Finding love in divine order

[1]There is therefore now no condemnation to them which are in Christ Jesus, who walk not after the flesh, but after the Spirit – Romans 8:1

As we find ourselves upon another Valentine's Day, there's a lot of talk about love out there. However, what I've often found is that if you dig deeper, there are as many people miserable around this time as there are that plan to be celebrating love. That's what makes love such a confusing thing. By definition, it's supposed to make everyone feel good. But love can make you miserable as well. While we like to see the wrong that happens in our lives as just the way things go sometimes, some misery comes to us by way of choice. And while love is an inexact science, we can increase our odds of success by seeking love in the right order.

Where we find ourselves getting confused is when we mix earthly things with divine happiness. Let me explain that one. We exist in the flesh, so we seek earthly things to make us happy. We seek earthly things to satisfy our flesh. We seek earthly things to "complete" us (that seems to be the popular phrasing these days). And while all of these things can satisfy us here on earth, they do nothing for your everlasting happiness. They do nothing for your divine happiness. We wind up doing things backwards. We seek to satisfy our flesh before we satisfy our souls.

What's most interesting to me is when we're out choosing our mates, rarely are we consulting God first. Now, I understand that that's not true with everyone reading this. There are plenty of you out there that seek the Father before you seek anything in your life, whether it's a job, a relationship or whatever. At the same time, I'm sure it wasn't always that way. I'm sure there was some trial and error that went on there. I know I've had my share of errors in my time. Those of us that have been around a day or two and fallen on our faces had to learn the hard way to leave it all to God.

When we find ourselves in bad relationships, we like to turn around and pretend that God is involved in every aspect of our lives. But it was you and only you that went out to the club and chose that woman or man in the midst of alcohol and bad decisions. It was you and only you that went against everything you were taught about what a good man or woman represents. And once things don't work out, you wanna give that person back to God. That's like me buying a brand new Toyota and once I realize that I'm unhappy with it, taking it back to the Dodge dealer. You didn't get that problem from here, so why are you looking to return it here? If God didn't give you that problem relationship, don't lay it at His feet and ask "Lord why?" He's been asking you why since you've been in that relationship.

Understand what I'm saying here. God is the solution to all of your problems, and that includes your love life. You can take your problems to God and allow Him to solve them for you. Just know that this was your doing and not His. Also, know that when you're off track with that part of your life, you may have made a wrong choice somewhere. You may have ignored a stop sign somewhere. That happens when we're trying to satisfy the flesh as opposed to doing things in divine order.

There are moments in our lives that are moments of clarity. There are certain moments that come along that put a lot of things into perspective. You can find yourself in a position where you realize that it's time to move on. But at the same time, you can find yourself in a position where you realize that you're right where you're supposed to be. While it's difficult to know which is which at any given time, it's not as difficult when you have placed all of your faith and trust in God and followed His direction.

This week, seek your love in divine order. Seek a love with God before you seek a love here on earth. The most important love that we can have in this life is love of God and love of self. If you don't have that, you can't successfully have any other kind of love. No matter what he promises, no matter what she says. No matter how much money he has, no matter how fine she is. If it isn't done in divine order, surely it will fall apart. But when it does, we can't fall apart with it. We must remember that God is the God of all things. He can solve your financial problems quicker than the state lottery. He can fix your misbehaving children quicker than boot camp or the court system. And yes, He can even solve your love life if you allow Him to. We must remember that God will give you the desires of your heart. The question that remains is, what does your heart desire?

A tribute to the virtuous woman

^{25}Strength and honour are her clothing; and she shall rejoice in time to come ^{26}She openeth her mouth with wisdom; and in her tongue is the law of kindness ^{27}She looketh well to the ways of her household, and eateth not the bread of idleness ^{28}Her children arise up and call her blessed; her husband also, and he praiseth her – Proverbs 31:25-28

Is there any greater blessing than a mother? I really don't know that there is. They are truly Heaven sent. No one loves like a mother. No one cares like a mother. No one makes you feel better when you're sick like mama. And most of all, no one understands like mama. She's the first one to yell at you when you do wrong and she's usually the last one to give up on you when you do. No matter how many times you stray from the path, when the whole world is against you, its mother that still stands by you. Yes, it's mother that will sometimes scream out in a crowd of naysayers, "Not my child", even though she may be dead wrong. Maybe because we've broken her heart with our wrongdoing. Or maybe because she's holding on to that last bit of hope that you followed what you were taught this time.

If your mother is anything like mine, she's a fountain of wisdom and knowledge. I try to drink from that fountain as often as I possibly can. While I didn't run wild in the streets as a youth, I was a little rebellious at times and disobeyed my mother. It took me some time, some mistakes and some life lessons learned before I realized that no one on this earth will ever love me the way that my dear mother does. And that's why we're best friends right now. She always listened when no one else would, she held my hand when I was afraid, she made me smile when I was down and she encouraged me when I had doubt. She's truly, truly one of a kind and I would be lost had I never had a mother like her.

While I understand that all mother/child relationships aren't the best, at some point in our lives, we've all benefited from knowing a great mother. Maybe she was in the church, maybe she was a school teacher or maybe she was just a concerned parent in the neighborhood. At some point in time, we were the recipient of a mother's love. The great men of the world know that love because they were molded by it. The virtuous women of the world were taught by them. Wherever you received that mother's love in your life, you must learn to appreciate it more than just once a year. You must appreciate it for a lifetime.

30Favour is deceitful, and beauty is vain: but a woman that feareth the Lord, she shall be praised – Proverbs 31:30

No one sacrifices like the real mothers in our lives. They will go hungry to feed their children. They'll sacrifice all that they have to make a better life for their children. I know this because I lived it. My mother was always there and I imagine, like Mary, she would be there until the end for any of her children. When Jesus was on His way to Calvary, it was Mary that walked the road with Him. Every step of the way. Whatever pain He felt, she felt it just the same. And she stayed with Him until He died. Then she took His body and laid it in that tomb. Only a mother could love her child that way.

This week, show your mother just how much you love and appreciate her. But don't just leave it at this Sunday. Just as she does with you, show her that love all year 'round. I understand that some of the people reading this email are without their mothers. Maybe she's already gone to meet God or maybe she's just not what she ought to be. That's okay because as I stated earlier, we all have a mother somewhere in our lives that deserves some credit for loving us and looking out for us.

If you can't reach your mom today, don't hold that love inside. Pass it on to the mothers that you can reach. In the event that you don't have that closeness with your mother, there's still time. To anyone out there that's a mother and you haven't done the best job, it's not too late. People may come and go in your children's lives, but one thing is for sure: No one can ever take your place. No one can ever replace your love. It truly is one of a kind and no one else can give it but you. You know how I know? My mama taught me that.

[10]Who can find a virtuous woman? For her price is far above rubies — Proverbs 31:10

Imperfection as the perfect example

[17]For I will restore health unto thee, and I will heal thee of thy wounds, saith the Lord... – Jeremiah 30:17

Check your body for scars right now. Go ahead, I'll wait. Some of you knew exactly where to look, while some of you had to search for a moment or two. Unless you're one of those people with an unusually scar free body, you found a few. What's most interesting about the scars that you see is the fact that you remember the circumstances in which they came about. In fact, with most scars, there's an interesting story behind it. Sometimes bad, sometimes scary and most certainly painful. But above all, they serve as reminders. They're reminders of how things can go wrong at times in your life.

Now, let's try a different exercise. Check your mind right now for mental scars. I won't wait for this one because we only have a few paragraphs together. These scars, though not visible, tend to be much more damaging than the physical scars that we have. The pain seems to be much deeper than those physical scars. Maybe because we can get rid of a lot of physical scars if we want to. But what's done to us mentally and emotionally can stay with us forever if we don't properly address it. How is it that life can be this way? Where the unseen can be more painful than what's seen?

In most cases, we become scarred because we've put ourselves in the wrong position in life. For the most part, scars seem to represent a mistake in our lives. If not a mistake, most certainly an unfortunate event. If you think about those physical scars, some were caused by being disobedient children and not listening to mom when she told you not to run so fast or not to ride your bike so recklessly. Been there, done that and my knees can prove it.

As far as the emotional scars, we can get those from being in the wrong relationships because we chose to ignore all of the signs that said this was wrong or we get them by not being where we're supposed to be in order to be in the right relationship and now we're filled with regret. Some may even be caused by family. But no matter the situation, circumstance or size and depth of the scar, rather than reliving the pain of it all, we can use that time in our lives for something more productive.

While the idea at times is to hide our scars because we may be ashamed of how we got them, it may be upon us to share some of the stories of those scars so that others may learn from them. I'm not suggesting that you put all of your business in the streets, but that which you can share, why not do so in order to keep someone else on the right path? If I can use my pain to help you avoid the same in life, why wouldn't I do it?

Based on something that happened in my family recently, I suggested that we do this more often with our children. Too often, we look at our scars and see them as no big deal because we survived them. So when our children are in a position to scar themselves, rather than protect them, we view their behavior as something we all must go through to grow. Where's the love? We must learn to give our children the benefit of our wisdom, not our foolishness. When we condone rather than correct, we become just as responsible for their behavior as they are.

While our children will no doubt make some of the same mistakes that we made as youths, the consequences for such acts are much greater for them than they were for us. Instead of reminiscing when we see them doing wrong – having flashbacks of our own youth and recklessness – we need to explain to them when they're off course because now that we see things through an adult's eyes, we can finally see what's wrong with the behavior. Hopefully. Just something to think about while we're telling everyone to lighten up and dismissing certain behavior as "kids being kids".

This week, don't be ashamed of your scars. Thank God that they've healed. And if they haven't quite healed, you can still go to Him and you will be healed. In my eyes, every scar that I have, both physically and mentally, is evidence of God and what He can do. I have been healed. And with that healing, I have chosen not to wallow in the circumstances of how I got my scars, but rather remind you weekly that God is able and He brought me out. Sure, the scar is the reminder, but the pain is all gone.

Week of September 5, 2010

An agent of change

[13] ...But Jesus said unto them, "A prophet is not without honour, save in his own country, and in his own house — Matthew 13:57

There were times when I questioned the journey I was on. When I decided to do what I do with The Weekly and teaching Bible class, I had a specific purpose in mind. I wanted to reach some people that were close to me. I felt that some of the people that I saw regularly could use my help, and I could use theirs. I thought if I studied and wrote it down and they read and gave me feedback, together we could all become closer to God. Together, we could all get a better understanding. In some ways, I've succeeded. But in other ways, no so much.

Naturally, when you've missed the target you were shooting for, you begin to question your aim. Did I miss or did the target move? But what I've learned is you need practice. In order to hit a target consistently, you must practice doing so. At times, that means practicing on targets that you may never consistently hit or may not hit at all. You practice just to get a rhythm to what you're doing. But sometimes, in the words of a song I know, ain't nothing wrong with your aim, you just gotta change the target.

So, if I ever thought I wasn't put here for change, I saw a glimpse of the truth yesterday. I was simply walking the street with my fiancée yesterday when a young man approached us as we were getting into the car. Naturally, in these days and times, I was on the defensive because a strange man approached. But he was sincere. He wanted to do us no harm. He simply saw something in me and wanted to ask a question.

He told me that I seemed as though I had myself together and he wanted to know how he could do the same. He explained to me that he was raised in the streets and he needed to know how he could go about changing himself in order to change his life. As many young people believe, he wanted to know if it was his appearance that was holding him back. Did the outside affect his inside?

I advised him that real change comes from the inside out. If he changes his mind, he can change his way of living. If he changes his mind, he could change his whole life. I advised him to start by treating people as he wants to be treated, with love and respect, and he could be on his way to real change. Material things don't matter until that first step is taken. Be beautiful on the inside and it will show on the outside. At that moment of advice that I gave, I realized what the target is.

The Word says that a prophet shall not be received in his own house. Now, I'm not suggesting that I'm a prophet. However, the way I see that verse, we are all here to spread the Word of God in some form or fashion and sometimes, those closest to us may tune a deaf ear to what we're saying. One of the reasons I was hesitant to step out and start doing what I've been doing is because I didn't think that people would listen to me. I felt that all of the people I knew that were close to me either weren't ready to hear what I had to say or wouldn't listen to me at all.

When you've known or think you've known a person in a certain capacity in your life, it's hard to change your mind about them. That is, unless you have a mind that's open to change. I imagine that some of the people that are close to me, but choose not to listen to what I'm saying have a hard time doing so because they only see me in that one capacity of their lives.

Their eyes and their minds won't allow them to see me any other way. But I can't allow that to be a deterrent. I can't allow that to cloud my vision. I can't allow that to stop me. My target isn't limited to those closest to me. My target is someone that doesn't know me. My target is someone that's lost in the world. My target is a strange man approaching me on the street because he may have seen a light inside me. My target is the world.

This week, whether you understand or not why God has called you to do something, do it anyway. Whether you think they care or not, do it anyway. Whether they accept it or not, do it anyway. We have to remember that God has His own reasons for sending us to do whatever it is He wants us to do. Sometimes we have enough vision and wisdom to see the big picture and what He's trying to do with us, and sometimes we don't. This is where your faith in God comes in. The work that God has for you to do, you must do. That's the message. I hear you, Lord.

June 24, 2008

"Let me tell you about the time I almost died…"

Have you ever felt like the world was just crashing in on you? Emotionally, professionally, spiritually and, of course, financially? Most of us can say that we've been there (or here if you're still there) before. It can be the most difficult and most devastating thing to ever happen to you, and sometimes all of those areas I mentioned will show up at once. You swim and you swim and you swim, but all that seems to do is prolong the inevitable. You seem to be sinking deeper and deeper. All of your problems daisy chained around your neck. You must face your untimely demise. The time has come to die.

As you may have noticed or figured out by now, I either survived or I have one hell of a crystal ball and I wrote this before I met my fate. I assure you it is the former and not the latter, but I gotta tell ya, it was close. Or at least it seemed that way. I recently went through a rough period in my life. As I've already stated, I know that I haven't cornered the market on such things. I was tested on many levels during this time, but more than anything, I felt that I was tested spiritually. Mind you, my faith in God never wavered and it never will. However, I feel that my spirit was tested.

When this happens in your life, you have to know the difference between your spirit being down and your faith in God being tested. Life has a way of doing this to you. I've often said that young people will sometimes have unrealistic views of life because the weight of the world hasn't crushed their spirit yet. It will happen to you. Sometimes, more than once in your life. But while your spirit may be down, you mustn't allow that to cause doubt in your mind about God. We're sometimes all too willing to place ourselves on the cross and scream out "Why has Thou forsaken me?" When the hour seems its darkest, we must maintain perspective.

I recently sat down with my son to discuss some troubles he was having in his life. Nothing major, but he's definitely helping to bring dad's spirit down and his stress level up. But that's life when you have a teenager. He's simply going through some of the things that teenagers go through. Peer pressure, the desire to test the parental boundaries and just the pains that come with trying to grow into an adult. One of the things that I told him was that part of being an adult is making individual decisions. I told him that he's coming to a point in his life when he has to make decisions based on what's best for him and his future and not so much about what his friends may think. It's amazing how the words you give to others are the very same words that can change your own life.

While some things that were going wrong in my life were simply some of the things that life puts you through, some of them were brought on by some of those individual choices that I made that weren't necessarily the best decisions. And while my faith in God hadn't been shaken, I wasn't communicating with Him the way that I should have been. I feel that He wanted my attention for some reason. Possibly to redirect my path again to what He would have me to do. I think I was hearing Him, but I wasn't listening.

Just when it seems that you're at your lowest, God will always send His angels to bring you out of whatever you're going through. For a while, I was quite distant and kept to myself. Some even suggested that I may have changed on them. To that I'll say, maybe you didn't know me as well as you thought. When I found myself wondering how I was going to make it, those angels found me. During those rare moments when I opened up to a few friends about what I was going through (I actually seem to be more willing to share with my website readers than people that I talk to daily; how twisted is that?), some of them were more than willing to lend an ear and be the support that I needed at the time. If you're reading this, you have my eternal gratitude.

But there was one angel in particular that made all the difference in the world. One night, while pumping that $4 per gallon gas into my gas guzzling Durango (that problem is almost gone), a woman at the gas station near my house approached me for change, as she often does anyone at that gas station. Before she could even finish her question, I hit her with the standard response, "Sorry, I don't have anything". As she began to walk away, she stopped and came back to me. She said, "You do have something. You have yourself and you have God. Have a blessed night".

As I finished pumping my gas, I reflected on what was just delivered to me, instantly reconnecting with my ability to recognize God's message, no matter what package it's delivered in. As I got back into my truck, I whipped around to the front of the gas station where that messenger was standing. I gave her the last $2 in my pocket. It may have meant some form of dinner to her that night, but I could never repay her for feeding my soul. What she gave me was worth far more than the $2 I gave her.

Not too long after that, I went to my spiritual advisor, my mom, and I had her pray for me. As we joined hands, she prayed a special prayer for her baby boy. A prayer so full of love, hope and promise that it had tears streaming down my face. As she wiped tears from my face, something that she's done so often throughout my life, she informed me that what she prayed for has already been done. "I know it's so", she said to me. "Your mama's prayers never go unanswered". As it is with anything else she says, I believe what my mama told me that night. Sometimes, in the midst of trouble in our lives, we need a reminder. Though the spirit may be weak at times, your strength remains in God. And with that said, let me rephrase the title of this piece. Let me tell you about the time God sent His angels to save me…

"My strength when I am weak..."

We're blessed so that we can bless

¹I love you, O LORD, my strength. ²The LORD is my rock and my fortress and my deliverer, my God, my rock, in whom I take refuge, my shield, and the horn of my salvation, my stronghold. – Psalm 18:1-2

Can I borrow $20? If we heard that question from a friend or family member, how many of us could handle the request without strain these days? If you can, you should consider yourself blessed. But how many of us that can do it, but with strain, consider ourselves blessed as well? Answer that within yourself as I continue.

These days, when someone asks us how we're doing, it seems that the thing to say is "I'm blessed". But do we truly mean it? Do we truly know what it means to be blessed? The truth is we're not always in tune with just how blessed we truly are. As we're all in the midst of financial turmoil, it may be difficult to be positive all the time. It's sometimes difficult to remember that your strength is in the Lord, and not in the almighty dollar, when every call is from a bill collector or a landlord. If you've ever been broke, you know how hard it is to smile when you're barely getting by. While you know that God is your rock, it's hard to ignore the fact that the car is on a ¼ tank, you need food for the house, pay day is still a week and a half away and you only have a $20 to your name. I guess that's why you need to borrow that $20 from me, right?

With the country in the financial state that it's in right now, we're all being tested. Some of us have lost jobs that we've had for years, if not, decades. Families have had to consolidate and move in together just to make ends meet. Houses continue to be foreclosed on, cars continue to be repossessed and we're all a little on edge. Those who have lost wonder how much more they can take or what's gonna happen next, while the rest wonder if they will be next. Even if you seem to have the most security on the job, you never really know. I mean, who knew just two years ago that the auto industry would be nearing extinction?

When you're struggling with life, as hard as it is, you must remember that you are still blessed. God has not left you. Having your will tested is just a part of life. You haven't lived if it's never happened to you. I'll often joke that young people run around as if they're invincible because the weight of the world hasn't crushed their spirit yet. However, this current climate that we're under knows no race, no class and no age. If you're not looking over your financial shoulder, there truly is something wrong with you. But in these times of trouble, you must take heed to the verse at the top of this page.

This week, when the hour seems it's darkest, read that verse. Though it's difficult to be positive when bills are piling up, doom and gloom is no way to live. While it's hard to smile through the pain sometimes, just remember that things will get better. It just takes a little time, a little patience and a lot of faith. At the same time, while it'd be great to sit back and wait for the government's bailout plans and rescue efforts, some out there need something right now. So if you know someone in need of that $20, dig deep if you can. It'll make you feel better to know that you've helped someone. Whether it feels like it or not, you are blessed.

Remaining faithful to the Lord

[14]*"Now therefore fear the LORD and serve Him in sincerity and in faithfulness. Put away the gods that your fathers served beyond the River and in Egypt, and serve the LORD.* [15]*And if it is evil in your eyes to serve the LORD, choose this day whom you will serve, whether the gods your fathers served in the region beyond the River, or the gods of the Amorites in whose land you dwell. But as for me and my house, we will serve the LORD." – Joshua 24:14-15*

This week, I came across a couple of situations that I'd like to share with you. This first situation consisted of an opportunity for financial growth by an individual. While it required nothing illegal, you could say that this individual would have had to sell out a little bit to gain this growth. In some ways, they would've had to sell their soul to get what they thought they really wanted. And while it seems that we always pray for financial growth, we must ask ourselves, is what we find ourselves chasing what God would have us to receive? Have you placed a price tag on your soul? In the end, are we praying for our own corruption? Marinate on that one for a second.

The second situation was a situation in which an individual seemed to be having all sorts of hardships in their lives. Now, as this information was being given to me, I must admit that some of it seemed a tad bit blown out of proportion. But we must remember that drama is in the eye of the beholder. What's a molehill to me may be a mountain to others. And while I sometimes know why that is, I still must remember to be sympathetic to others. Now, I'm not one that claims to have all of the answers. However, my position is like that of a woman that's shoe shopping on a budget. While she may not be able to afford all of the latest fashions, she still knows where to find them. And while I may not have all the answers, I do know where to find them. Sometimes, in the game of life, we just gotta hit the reset button.

This week's verse seems to speak to both these situations. On the one hand, when we look at the shape that our country and our economy's in, we sometimes wonder what happened and where we went wrong. But the 14th verse says it all. As a country, we've found ourselves serving the gods of our fathers. War and money. And because money seems to be the problem, we automatically assume that money is the only solution. While more money definitely would help, is that where our focus should immediately shift or should we allow God to work this out as He sees fit? We have to understand that we can't serve two gods. Believe it or not, we've driven a wedge between ourselves and God in this country.

Now, once we've driven this wedge between ourselves and God, Satan has a doorway in which to make his way into our lives. So, even the slightest difficulties in our lives seem to be too much to bear. We fall apart as if we have no idea what to do, where to go or whom to turn to. We find ourselves staying home from church and feeling sorry for ourselves. Now, instead using the Word of God to break up that weekly secular circle that we often find ourselves in, we allow it to go on and on and on, with no end in sight. Once you lose that connection with God, it can appear that all is lost. This is why we must serve the Lord in sincerity and faithfulness. We don't half step when we sin, so we shouldn't half step with God.

This week, make sure that you make your connection with God. This is where all of your strength comes from. In that second situation, I discovered that this individual hadn't been to church as they should. The thing is, when we miss out on church, not only have we disobeyed God, but we also miss out on what we need to get through the week. We miss out on blessings. Contrary to popular belief, all of our blessings do not come just from tithing and they are not all material. Therefore, we must refrain from bowing in submission to those material gods. Good health is a blessing. Patience is a blessing. Having enough to cover your bills is a blessing. But blessings also come with giving of your self in service to God. And we must serve Him faithfully. After a week under attack from the enemy, we need to be refreshed. We need to be reminded that we can go on. Know that you can conquer life and all of its trials. God has not left you. Just make your way to the House of The Lord and hit the reset button.

Week of March 15, 2009

Your strength has been renewed!

[28] Have you not known? Have you not heard? The LORD is the everlasting God, the Creator of the ends of the earth. He does not faint or grow weary; his understanding is unsearchable. [29] He gives power to the faint, and to him who has no might he increases strength. [30] Even youths shall faint and be weary, and young men shall fall exhausted; [31] But they who wait for the LORD shall renew their strength; they shall mount up with wings like eagles; they shall run and not be weary; they shall walk and not faint. – Isaiah 41:28-31

As the saying goes, a chain is only as strong as its weakest link. While this is true in terms of the chain, this has also served as a metaphor for life. I've seen this play out in the black community on a regular basis. We sometimes fall short because we fail to provide strength to that weakest link. We become broken as a community because we're only concerned with our own individual strength. We lose sight of the fact that if our brothers and sisters have fallen, we have fallen too.

However, the weakest of us isn't something that's easily identified. For example, if I have a chain with a link that's weak, it's upon me to strengthen that link. Once I do that, another link invariably becomes the weakest link. This is how we are in life. There is no one weakest link. On any given day, we may find ourselves in that role. I've often felt that God has placed me in certain positions so that I might provide strength to others. But at any time, we are all susceptible to the ups, downs, ins and outs of life. At any give moment, our circumstances may have us down on our knees.

This week has been an interesting one. As I've heard from some of you, it seems that we've all had some sort of trials this week. Moments of weakness, if you will. While some of us struggled with some personal issues, some of us were struck with the two things that we all have to deal with, no matter race, color or creed: death and finances. These are things that can make you feel as if you've hit rock bottom, especially considering who you may have lost or how much you stand to lose.

To those in despair, I know you're down. But when you gon' get up? You ain't heard? There is no end to what God can do. The devil is strong, but we're stronger. We have to fight back. As some of you have been tried by the fire this week, this is your reminder. No matter what may have happened, your help is always there. We as humans have limitations to what we can do and how much we can take from life. But our strength comes from the Lord and there's no end to what He can do. As the verse says, you just have to wait on Him, and though you may be weary, your strength will be renewed.

This week, when you're feeling as though you're that weak link in the chain, do not be discouraged. I'm reminded of that old spiritual that says "I'm so glad trouble don't last always". Your trials are only temporary. Though you may feel the weight of your current situation is too much to bear, God is waiting to re-energize you. He's waiting to give you another dose of power. He's waiting to give you the wings of an eagle so that you can fly. Have you not known? Have you not heard? God is alive and your strength has been renewed.

Week of March 22, 2009

Turning tears of sorrow to tears of joy

[5] *"Those who sow in tears shall reap with shouts of joy! [6] He who goes out weeping, bearing the seed for sowing, shall come home with shouts of joy, bringing his sheaves with him." - Psalm 126:5-6*

In my next book, I spent half a chapter on Hurricane Katrina and the effect it had on my life. Although I wasn't a personal victim of the Hurricane, it still had a profound effect on me. Now, it may seem like old news now, but let me bring some perspective to the situation. If you as a black person have ever discussed race with a white person, you can feel the tension. If the white person is in no way, shape or form a racist individual, they're still uncomfortable when we speak about the atrocities committed against our people by their people. They almost seem to wanna hug you and say "it'll be okay".

However, if you still seem to be angry or hurt about what happened 40 or 50 years ago, they seem to give you a look that suggests, "C'mon, that was so long ago. You should get over it". How does this relate to Hurricane Katrina, you ask? Well, the moral here is a tragedy that may seem like a long time ago to someone on the outside looking in, can still feel like yesterday to someone still living it. While some may have pushed Hurricane Katrina to the backs of their minds, there are some people out there that are still dealing with this tragedy.

Now, as far as tragedies go, it's usually in the eye of the beholder. What's a big deal to you may not be a big deal to me, and vice versa. Something like New Orleans or racism shows us what real tragedies look like. Conversely, we will take something that in no way, shape or form compares to something as significant as those two things or something like them, and make a big deal out of it. We take life's minor inconveniences and make them major events. And when something does qualify as a big deal, we act as though our house is under water and we've lost everything.

But what we all should've learned from the people of New Orleans is a lesson in survival. What they should've taught us is that we are not our possessions. The people that love us are the ones that keep us going. What keeps us going is a merciful God. No matter what you have or don't have, you are still better off than someone else out there. No matter what possessions you may gain or lose in this life, just being alive to feel the pain, anger, anguish or whatever you may feel about the situation is a blessing. And though we may get emotional about the situation, we must regain perspective. Though sometimes we may lose in life, we can still win with God!

In the past week, I've personally seen proof of how God can bless you. He has brought Sunshine to my cloudy days. I believe He can do the same for you. This week's verse speaks to the things we may go through in life that bring us to tears. While so many of us want our lives to be full of good times, we're sometimes unwilling to deal with life on life's terms. There will be some bad times. But it's what you do with those tears that you cry that makes all the difference. Sometimes, you can lose your place in this world. You can get so caught up in what you have, what you don't have, what hasn't been given to you and what's been taken away from you. We can't allow ourselves to be ruled by our circumstances. When the devil seeks to defeat you, God has already got your next victory lined up.

This week, when life gives you tears of sorrow, you must plant them into fertile ground immediately. Don't dwell on your problems, seek out solutions. And once you have that solution, don't regress to a place of sorrow and begin wallowing in self-pity again. Thank God for answering your prayers, let go of the pain and move on. God is able to turn those tears of sorrow into joy. It's easy to remain in a state of anger, frustration and sadness. But you can never heal if you don't take your troubles to God and lay them down, never to pick them up again. Take my word for it, when one door closes, another opens. You just have to be willing to do what

The Word says. If New Orleans can smile through the pain, we should all have hope.

Week of March 29, 2009

Finding joy inside your tears

³¹Let all bitterness and wrath and anger and clamor and slander be put away from you, along with all malice. ³²Be kind to one another, tenderhearted, forgiving one another, as God in Christ forgave you. – *Ephesians 4:31-32*

If you've ever come in contact with a person that's bitter or angry about their past, you know what an unpleasant experience it can be. They're all too willing to tell you why they're mad, hurt, disappointed or whatever, but they're so reluctant to let it go. They wear their pain like a badge of honor. You wanna sympathize with them, but at the same time, you wonder how a person can be so miserable over something that may have happened years ago.

One of the most difficult things to do is to let go of the past. We carry the hurt and the pain of our pasts from year to year and relationship to relationship. Never really realizing how much damage we do to our current and future situations, we carry those heavy bags of misery along with us throughout our lives. While it's easy to see how this can complicate things in our love lives, this can also affect us in other aspects of life. It affects how we live and it affects how we interact with others.

Everything in life is more difficult when you have no peace within. As this week's verse suggests, we should be kind and tenderhearted to one another. This includes those that may have done us wrong. We all struggle with this from time to time because sometimes others can really hurt us deeply. But a spirit of forgiveness is so necessary in our lives. While sometimes this can be difficult depending on what we're being asked to forgive, it is something that we all must learn to do. We can't treat forgiveness as an option. It's what you must do. God cannot forgive us for our sins if we refuse to forgive one another. We're not always aware that we sometimes can't move forward with our lives because we can't forgive. We remain trapped in the past.

We can delay God's blessings by holding on to the negative. Better jobs are out there. Better relationships with your family are out there. True love is out there. But you gotta let go of your past in order to embrace your future. It's easy to say that you've moved on from a particular situation, but have you really forgiven those that may have done you wrong? I can personally testify to the fact that life is so much better when you let it go and forgive. You have no idea about the blessings that are waiting for you. Unlike those that live in the night time of their pain from day to day, my Sunshine gets brighter and brighter as my life goes on.

This week, search your heart for those things in your past that are still haunting your today. Search for those things in your right now that are threatening your future. Seek them out and eliminate them today. God is ready to replace all of your bitterness and anger with joy. There's a better job on the way. There's a better relationship with your kids on the way. There's a better relationship with your family on the way. There's even real love on the way. Put your bags down now. Pick up your brand new day on your way out the door. We all know that God is able. The question that remains is, are you?

Week of April 12, 2009

Have the courage to be patient

[14]Wait on the LORD: be of good courage, and He shall strengthen thine heart: wait, I say, on the LORD – Psalm 27:14

Sometimes on our jobs, we either have to delegate things out or we have something delegated to us by our superiors. Usually, this is done because a job needs to be done, but someone's plate is full. However, sometimes it's done because one person simply can't handle the job and needs a more experienced hand to tackle the situation. But in some situations, we're not in a position of delegation. We sometimes have to ask someone with more experience to help us with something. We all have the ability to save ourselves rather than holding out for a hero, but the fact is, sometimes, we just need someone else to take the reigns.

The only problem with having something delegated to you is when it comes from someone that micromanages. If you have the time to stand over my shoulder every step of the way in an effort to make sure I do what you want me to do, exactly as you say I should do it, then why not simply do it yourself and save us both some time? When you're passing work along to the next person, you should be passing it to someone that you trust to do the job, whether you're around or not. But when you're asking for help from a higher authority, your mentality should be different.

For example, if you find yourself in a tight spot, and you have to go to mom, dad, sister, brother or friend for financial help, it would be wise to not tell them how they should help you and how quickly they should move on this. You can't put yourself in the position of one who delegates when you're actually in need of help. This is where we find ourselves with God at times. We have yet to learn how to lay our troubles down at the altar and leave them there. Thus, we continue to stress over them long after we have supposedly let them go.

When we're faced with life's trouble, we often call on the Lord to save us. We swear that we've turned things over to God, and yet we continue to meddle in His business. We have forgotten how to pray in this life. "Lord, if it's Your will…" should always be your prayer. Not, "Lord, I need Your blessing, and here's how we'll do it…" If you've got all of the answers, then what do you need God for? When you turn things over to God, you have to have the right mentality. When you turn things over to God, it becomes His business and His business alone. You must remember that you are no longer in charge of this. You have not delegated this out. You have asked the Almighty for His assistance. You must remember that you cannot micromanage God.

This week, we need to practice what the verses are saying to the tee. Wait on the Lord. The verse at the top of this page is one of my mother's favorites. She often tells us to wait on the Lord. God will always show up on time. He's never, ever late. No matter what you're looking for in your life, He will deliver it at the right time. Not when you want it, but when it's time. Those that oppose us and wish ill of us can do nothing about it. It's already written.

So often, we aren't ready for the blessings that we're asking for and this is what causes the "delay", if you will. Sometimes we're not right in our spirit and whether we realize that or not, God does. We have an inheritance to gain if we simply show patience and wait for God to bless us. Before you know anything, your spiritual life will be better. Your finances will work out. That perfect love that you've finally decided to stop chasing and let God deliver to you may wind up sitting right next to you. That job that you've searched high and low for will come calling on your phone asking you what time you can be there. It's been said over and over in these emails. God is able even when we aren't. And contrary to popular belief, He doesn't need you looking over His shoulder to make sure He's getting it done. All of the desires of your heart that are within His will are waiting for you. Will you wait on the Lord?

[34]Wait on the LORD, and keep His way, and He shall exalt thee to inherit the land: when the wicked are cut off, thou shalt see it. — Psalm 37:34

Week of April 26, 2009

Trained to defeat the enemy

[31] ...Satan hath desired to have you, that he may sift you as wheat – Luke 22:31

If any of you live here in Michigan or have lived here, you know how bad the roads can be. Potholes and such that could swallow a small child completely. And knowing that, you know what kind of damage they can do to your car when you don't see them coming. But those of us that are careless will drive over potholes at normal speed and do all kinds of damage to our rides. While the damage can be repaired, it can also be costly. Where we could've simply slowed down and eased through that rough patch in the road and saved ourselves time, energy and money, we rushed through without any regard for what may happen. It's funny how life can mirror these horrible Michigan roads.

Last week, it seemed as if the devil had attempted to lie down a few of his personal potholes in my path. He tried a little harder than normal to steal my joy. But this is no surprise to me. When you try to walk in the will of God, he always tries harder. We talked recently in an email about the joy that God gives us. But the devil is reading my emails, too. And if he's not on the mailing list, he may be getting them forwarded to him. But make no mistake about it, he's quite aware of what I've been doing. He's quite aware of some of the things that God has done in my life since the beginning of the year. He's quite aware of the blessings I have received. He's quite aware of the happiness I've found. He's quite aware of the peace that I'm feeling. He's also aware of the changes God has made in me. And he's not pleased about any of it.

We can never doubt the devil's presence in our lives. What that means is that we must slow down and take notice of him or he will damage you like potholes to your front end. If not monitored, he can pose a real threat to your happiness.

Success on your job? He comes to bring disharmony in the workplace. Newfound success in your marriage or your relationships? He sends people to sow seeds of discord due to the fact that their jealous and wished they had what you have. Your family trying to come together after years of dysfunction? He reminds you of the old arguments that separated you in the first place so that you can go back to square one.

We have to remember that while the devil is aware and most times the cause of your failures in life, he's also more acutely aware of your successes. And he seeks to turn those into failures. When we seek that stronger relationship with God and ourselves, we must remember that the devil sees that as a challenge. He sees it as an opportunity to prove himself. He'll do that by attempting to steal your joy. He'll try to show you that things aren't going as well as you think they are.

[13]For such are false apostles, deceitful workers, transforming themselves into the apostles of Christ [14]And no marvel; for Satan himself is transformed into an angel of light – 2 Corinthians 11:13-14

He will also send his army to destroy what you're building in your new life. However, you can't always recognize them when they come. They come dressed as well wishers. They come dressed as family. They come dressed as friends. And they come in all ways, shapes, sizes and forms. While we'd always like to simply say to the devil, "Get thee behind me", we must understand that sometimes, dealing with the devil and his foolishness takes time. We have to slow down and handle that bit of business.

This week, if the devil wants to fight you, take him on. This is what I've chosen to do when he tries to take me out. But if you're fearful of the battle, let me ease your mind. You must remember that you're a child of God, armed with the Word of God. Through that Word, you have been given extensive training. If you haven't gone through training, then use that Word as a training manual and get ready for war. But know this. God has given us enough in strength and courage to go 15 rounds with Lucifer, if that's what he wants to do. If you truly know the Lord, you mustn't be afraid and you shouldn't be surprised. The devil's attacks are part of the road to salvation. If he wants to fight, then we have to be ready. And I don't know about you, but I never lose.

Week of May 3 2009

Everything is not worth your tears

⁹And He said unto me, My grace is sufficient for thee: for my strength is made perfect in weakness. Most gladly therefore will I rather glory in my infirmities, that the power of Christ may rest upon me ¹⁰Therefore I take pleasure in infirmities, in reproaches, in necessities, in persecutions, in distresses for Christ's sake: for when I am weak, then am I strong - 2 Corinthians 12:9-10

When life gives you lemons, make lemonade. Or throw them at the people trying to force their lemons on you. Okay, let's not get off track. This is not what The Weekly is all about. But it is all about helping us to overcome life's little tragedies and appreciate the good things. But sometimes, this is easier said than done. We talked last week about how the devil can get involved and mess up a whole bunch of things. So what can we do with ourselves when it's not so much about what the devil is doing, but more so about what life is doing to us?

If you're over the age of 21 and you have real responsibility in your life, you probably realize by now that life isn't as easy as you thought it would be. Jobs are challenging, relationships are challenging, friendships are challenging, and trying to keep up your end of the bargain as it relates to your relationship with God is definitely challenging. So when life is dealing out disappointments quicker than a Las Vegas blackjack dealer, you're not in the mood to say "hit me". Sometimes, you just wanna break down and cry. Let me tell you why you shouldn't.

While we all have been in situations where we're so mad, frustrated, disappointed or whatever, that we wanted to cry, we have to be stronger than that situation that we find ourselves in. Your relationship with God should be the foundation to all that you do in your life. That should be your source of strength to carry on and go through any situations that you may be facing. You can look at the news everyday and see how this current financial "crisis" has taken its toll on society. People are killing themselves, and in some cases, their families over losing their jobs and their so-called fortunes. In my mind, only a person that doesn't really know God and what He's capable of can have an outlook on life that's so bleak, that they're willing to do such things.

As Christians, the only real crisis that we should ever face is being in danger of going to hell. We already know that our fortune exists in Heaven. My mom and I recently chuckled about the current financial struggles the nation is facing. We laughed at the fact that this is nothing new for Black people, and we'll be fine. Simply put, we've had to survive on little to nothing in the past and we can do it again. In the cotton fields, we had nothing but one another and God. Those of us that never lost that mentality will still be here when the economy turns around.

Recently, we here at KJWorldOnline.com have started a bi-weekly round table. We get together and discuss things that we may be going through in our lives and try to help each other navigate through life a little more smoothly. As we were talking this past weekend, we began discussing a past email I sent out where I reminded everyone that we are not our possessions in life, and we are not our circumstances. And when these circumstances get to be too much or we find ourselves without the possessions in life that we deem necessary, we can't always give in to our emotions. I reminded everyone at that table that everything is not worth your tears.

This week, I want you all to remember where your strength lies. When you feel like giving in to those tears, hold back. If you're not strong enough, call for back up. Ask God for an extra dose of strength. Don't cry over your job. Thank God that you have one. Don't cry over lost friendships. There's no friend like Jesus. Don't cry over failed relationships. If it was meant to be and it was ordained by God, it will still be. And if it wasn't, God's got something better in store for you. Don't cry over finances. Get with my Daddy, because He owns all of this.

Unlike Johnson and Johnson's, God's promise of no more tears is real. God can actually deliver on His promise in Philippians 4:19 to "supply all of your needs according to His riches in Glory". Instead of crying about it, let's try something new. How 'bout shouting for joy. Now, stop worrying about your troubles, go out and have a glass of lemonade.

Down, but not defeated

[8]We are troubled on every side, yet not distressed; we are perplexed, but not in despair; [9]Persecuted, but not forsaken; cast down, but not destroyed –
II Corinthians 4:8-9

Our goals in life vary from person to person. Some of us want to be doctors and lawyers. Some of us want to work diligently in the community to make our neighborhoods better places to live. Some of us want to be famous and some of us what to do great things while remaining anonymous. But no matter what we may wanna do or be in our lives, ultimately all of us just wanna be happy. But sometimes, life gets in the way.

There are times in life when it becomes quite a struggle to keep our particular circumstances from getting us down. When the rent's due, the car note's due and the kids need things, all from a paycheck that would only cover one or two of those things at best, it's hard to keep from going crazy. When your friends seem to be turning their backs on you at a rapid pace or your seemingly great relationship seems not so great anymore, it's hard to keep your head up and your eyes free from tears. But there are reasons why you must.

First things first, we all must learn to identify those components that contribute to real happiness in our lives. Too often we find ourselves wrapped up in people and things that bring us temporary joy, but doesn't necessarily make us continuously happy. We have songs that talk about not being happy or not knowing joy until a certain status in life or a certain individual came along. We embrace phrases like "you complete me" or "you make me whole". While those sentiments are nice, are they really a healthy mindset to have about someone that exists in the flesh just as you do?

We often make life more difficult than it has to be. For example, the clothes, the car notes and the homes that I mentioned earlier are just a fact of life. But do they exist in excess because of hard times and job loss or because we're living above our means? It has been man's custom to dig himself into a deep hole, and then fall to his knees and pray like he's never prayed before. We always do this in times of trouble, but never in thanks and recognition of times of peace. We're blessed to serve a God that doesn't hold grudges as we do.

As for our relationships, is that friendship struggling because you placed more stock in a person than you should have when there was evidence that suggested this was more of an acquaintance than a friend? Have you unfairly placed the burden of your happiness onto your significant other? We should never make another responsible for our complete happiness. True love, happiness and friendship are rare, and thus hard to find. But that's what makes them so special. If it weren't this way, all of these things would lose their value because everyone would be in a constant state of bliss. So you must first make yourself happy because others should only contribute to what you already have. Only God can "complete you" or "make you whole".

It's been said that only the strong survive, but that isn't always true. The weak survive in this life as well. The difference is the strong know what to do when they feel themselves getting weak. The strong know where their strength can be renewed. The weak can survive, but they often live in misery. They often live in a state of uncertainty. They have no idea what tomorrow will bring. But we don't have to exist in such a way. We don't have to live as the weak do. We have a source of strength that we can turn to.

How many times has God let you down? I'll answer for you: never! We often confuse a rough patch in our lives with real trouble. But there's nothing happening down here that we can't overcome. There's nothing going on down here that we haven't already overcome. It's all in how you see things. It's all based on you relationship with The Almighty. You can maintain perspective in life. You can maintain happiness in your life. Often, I'm asked why I never worry. Outside of the fact that my mother taught me to never do so, I don't know why any Christian ever should. That isn't to suggest that we never have situations come about in our lives that may cause us to do so, but I contend that only those that don't know God will remain in such a state.

This week, be reminded of who you are. Remind yourself of where you come from. Most importantly, when you feel as though you're at your end, remind yourself of where your strength comes from. Keep this week's verse on your mind. No matter your circumstances, you are not defeated. You are not forsaken, neither are you destroyed. You are not distressed nor are you in despair. Whether it be a bad day at the office or a bad day at home. Whether it be a broken friendship, a broken relationship or broken finances. As the verse suggests, all of these are temporary conditions. Yes, fall to your knees and take your troubles to God. But when you get up, get up with renewed strength. Get up with a purpose. Get up with faith and confidence in what you've just done. And most of all, get up without your problems and be ready to live out His solutions.

A test of your faith

[19]And when He (Jesus) saw a fig tree by the wayside, He came to it and found nothing thereon, but leaves only. And He said unto it, "Let no fruit grow on thee henceforward forever." And immediately the fig tree withered away. [20]And when the disciples saw it, they marveled, saying, "How soon has the fig tree withered away!" [21]Jesus answered and said unto them, "Verily I say unto you, if ye have faith and doubt not, ye shall not only do this which is done to the fig tree, but also if ye shall say unto this mountain, `Be thou removed and be thou cast into the sea,' it shall be done. [22]And all things whatsoever ye shall ask in prayer, believing, ye shall receive." – Matthew 21:19-22

I have faith in these desolate times. There I go quoting songs that only I may know, but this is the mentality that I must have. While it can be difficult to maintain this mindset with all that we deal with on a day to day basis, having anything less than faith that things will always get better will drive you crazy. Most of us have had moments in our lives where we felt like our "faith" was being tested. While that may be a popular phrase to use from time to time, is it really an appropriate one? Though you may feel that way at times, is it the faith that's the issue or the things that you put your faith in? Think about that one.

Now, if we're talking about things of an everyday, worldly nature, then I understand. When you watch people being fired and/or laid off on your job on a regular basis, it's easy to not have complete faith in your job. When lies and infidelity began to seep into your relationship, having less faith in what you have makes sense. When every secret that you've shared with a close friend or family member always seems to find it's way to the grapevine, then it makes sense to wonder who you can put your faith and trust in.

If you've ever broken up with someone, fell out with friends or family members or even lost a job before, sometimes in the heat of the moment, you'll throw blame around in every direction but your own. But eventually, after some time has passed, most of us will look back on the situation and see where we could've done better. We'll look back and see where either ourselves or both parties involved may not have been completely invested and fully committed to what it took to make the relationship work.

Putting aside the fact that there are instances where it may have been only one person's fault or the fact that this may be being read by some of those perfect people that walk amongst us and never do any wrong, we also face certain situations in life from time to time where it just wasn't meant to be. At the same time, if you don't have complete faith in something, how long will it really last anyway?

What never makes sense to me is when those of us that say we're Christians get to a point where we say that our faith in worldly things is being "tested". I gave some examples of some man made situations that could easily falter. Those situations are not based in anything that would last forever. All earthly things will fall apart, sometimes without a moment's notice. Those situations are like the fig tree and may have bee pre-ordained to wither away and die. But we have to remember that we are in a relationship with God and relationships are a two-way street. All parties have to do their part. I'm so sure that God is always doing His part. In fact, I have complete faith in that fact. The question is, are we doing ours? When we place our ultimate faith in God, how could worldly situations ever give us tests that we can't pass?

If we're really connected with God, our faith should never be shaken. This is a difficult mentality to attain, but far from an impossible one. This isn't to suggest that the devil won't come, but if your mind is focused on God and what He has for you, the devil can't break you. The problem that we have sometimes is that faith requires a few things from us that we're not always willing to provide. Faith requires commitment. You must commit yourself to God to the same degree that you'd like for Him to commit to you. Faith requires work. You must be making every attempt to live right in His sight daily.

Faith requires belief in the unseen. Once you do those things, as the verse says, you must believe that what you ask for in prayer, you will receive. Not according to your watch, but according to His.

This week, when you feel that your faith is being tested, do some self examination and ask, "Where have I placed my faith?" If you examine yourself and you're truly doing as you should, then you must wait on The Lord in times of trouble. Too often we look to God to save us from a particular situation or moment in our lives, when in fact we're looking to Him to save us from ourselves. But you can't cry out to God to save you if you insist on living outside of His will. Yes, we can move mountains with our faith. Yes, what we ask for in prayer, if we believe, He will grant it. But you must be in position to receive those blessings. You must be committed to the relationship. And in the most desolate of times, you must have faith.

Week of September 6, 2009

Stepping out on faith

¹Now faith is the substance of things hoped for, the evidence of things not seen – Hebrews 11:1

Missed opportunities are a part of life. All of us can think back to a moment in our lives when we let a golden opportunity slip by. Give it some thought right now. If you can't think of a moment where you missed an opportunity to do something in your life and it caused you a little regret, you have led a remarkable life. Or maybe you're one that doesn't regret very much in life. Anyway, no matter the reason you let the moment pass you by, we've all sat around wondering "what if" about certain things in life. Whether it's a big opportunity or something small, it's always a nagging and uncomfortable feeling thinking about "the one that got away". Some of us simply move on, while others are forever caught in that moment.

Most times when we think of "the one that got away", we're thinking of things of a romantic nature. A relationship that ended before we thought it should have or one that never started for whatever reason. But there are other opportunities that we miss out on that have nothing to do with our romantic lives. It could've been a job opportunity, an opportunity to go to school or an opportunity to live out a dream. But, is all ever really lost? While some things in life are once in a lifetime, in a lot of cases, we're given a second chance. In fact, some opportunities aren't completely gone and we still have time to take advantage. It's all in how you look at things

What I've found is that some of the opportunities that we miss out on, we do so out of fear. Traveling into the unknown takes a lot of courage. At the same time, there's a thin line between bravery and stupidity. But where it may seem that we're doing the smart thing by playing it safe and sticking to safer territories, we're sometimes selling ourselves short. Sure, we'd all take advantage of a lot of things if we only had some assurances that things would work out. It's that fear of the unknown that causes us to be hesitant.

For example, we don't commit to certain relationships because we aren't sure that the person we're committing to is The One. We won't leave other relationships because we're afraid of being alone and we don't know when we'll find someone else. We don't take a chance on a particular job offer because we don't know for sure that we'll be secure there. We won't leave others because we don't know if we can find another job in time to keep the bills from piling up. But sometimes, these things aren't simply a matter of bravery or stupidity. Sometimes, in order to take advantage of a chance that life is giving you, you have to just step out on faith.

Personally, I find myself on this road today. I feel that I have to step out on that faith and do something different in my life. And while there may have been a time in my life where I might have been hesitant or would rather play it safe, that mentality doesn't exists in me right now. To quote another song I know, "there's someone else I've got to be". I feel that I'm being given another opportunity to do something great. I've been given the opportunity to do something special. This time, I'll make it happen.

As we've discussed in these emails before, there is a calling on all of our lives. There's a responsibility that we all have to live up to our potential. This may require us to do things that are a bit uncomfortable for a while. It may cause us to make some unpopular decisions. It may cause us to lose a friend or two along the way. In reality, it sounds just like what we have to do when we accept Christ as our savior. But more than anything, it requires faith. Faith in yourself, faith in your abilities and faith that as long as you're in the will of God, He won't let you fail. You do your job and I'm sure He'll do His.

This week, eliminate your fear and step out on faith. Too often, we allow fear to keep us from the things that we really want in life. But we shouldn't exist in that mindset. God has so much more in store for us. Whatever your calling is in life, this is your opportunity to live it out. And there are many ways in which God places a calling on our lives. Helping in the community could be a calling on your life. Adopting children can be a calling on your life. Helping others to improve their lives could be a calling on your life. Even becoming President could be a calling on your life. There are soldiers for the cause in every walk of life. We simply have to have faith in what we're called to do and be willing to walk the path that God has set for us. I can see my next opportunity for greatness. And this time, I won't miss it. What about you?

6But without faith, it is impossible to please Him: for he that cometh to God must believe that He is, and that He is a rewarder of them that diligently seek Him – Hebrews 11:6

Week of October 4, 2009

Staying on the divine course

[17]No weapon that is formed against thee shall prosper; and every tongue that shall rise against thee in judgment thou shalt condemn. This is the heritage of the servants of the Lord, and their righteousness is of me, saith the Lord – Isaiah 54:17

This week has been an interesting one. It started with several emails from a lot of you telling me how much you enjoyed last week's email, and I thank you for that. You are all an inspiration to me. However, it ended with someone seemingly questioning my work and what I do. Now, this could all be that infamous KJ paranoia creeping in, but I'm usually pretty accurate when it comes to stuff like that. But more than that, I'm usually undeterred as well. I'm much stronger than any doubt the devil attempts to bring my way. From that, I have a new motto: This is not an image. This is God-given.

Unfortunately, anytime you're trying to do something positive in life, there's always going to be some negativity on the other side of that. It's just a part of life. It doesn't make sense, but it is what it is. I could write a hundred of these emails and someone will always want to talk about the things that I've done in my past, as if they are without sin. You could go out tomorrow and feed a thousand hungry people at a soup kitchen and all someone will wanna talk about is the fact that you had children out of wedlock. You could go door to door trying to draw souls to Christ and all someone will wanna talk about is the fact that you weren't always like that. The energy they could be using to make their own mark in the world, they're using to try and bring you down.

When we see things like this in our lives, we must remember that we're cut from a different cloth. We must remember that we're stronger than any adversity that we ever face here on earth. For example, I'm often questioned indirectly on my job about why I don't, for lack of a better term, show more fear when it comes to the higher ups and when it comes to job security. Call me crazy, but the notion that I should fear anyone on this earth is offensive to me. While we all need jobs and we have people in positions of authority on our jobs, none of this warrants my fear. Only God can have that effect on me. The same can be said for anyone that feels that what I'm doing here lacks merit or sincerity. Believe it or not, this is my destiny.

All of us have a path that we're supposed to be on in life. All of us have a destiny. While some may suggest that we create these things on our own, I completely disagree. This is where I feel that man allows his arrogance to overshadow what God has designed. We struggle to acknowledge God when we arrive at a place of peace in our lives. We'd rather say we created it as opposed to believing that we simply found what God already had waiting for us. We are all created by God with a purpose. As we are led by Him, we can find that purpose in life. Thus, you find yourself. It's when we stray from that path that we end up lost. And while some may desire to question my words, that is your prerogative. But I assure you, I am far from lost.

This week, don't allow the devil to question your path. Seek your destination as guided by God. I heard a saying not too long ago: What you will do eventually, you should do immediately. So what that means for me is that I'm following what I feel is the voice of God leading me further into the greatness that He's promised to all of us. What you do in your life, you must do to please God. We can't do the things that we do to please man because man is ever changing, but God is the same yesterday, today and forever. As long as your soul is aligned with the Heavens above, you will reach your destination in life. God has already directed my path. I have another motto: I'm already great. And so are you as long as you believe.

Remaining centered

[39]But the salvation of the righteous is of The Lord; He is their strength in the time of trouble. [40]And The Lord shall help them, and deliver them...
– Psalm 37:39-40

We often hear talk of staying centered or grounded. What does that really mean and how do we accomplish that when there's so much in our lives that can throw us off the path? How do you keep your cool when every bill you have is either due or past due? How do you stay calm when your kids seem intent on being disobedient? How do you keep your composure when loneliness seems to have settled into your life after your relationship has fallen apart? How do you stay focused on the positive when negativity is constantly staring you right in the face? There is a way.

Too often, we allow our situations to take us so far away from where we need to be, that we can hardly find our way back. Whether you're a person of faith or not, you can find yourself in a position where you wanna throw up both your hands, Marvin Gaye style, and just give up. It seems to be the easiest thing to do because you feel lost. But you'll never get home that way. And in this day and age of navigation this and GPS that, how could anyone ever get lost anyway? But if you just keep your bearings and take a look around in your life, I'm sure you'll start to notice some pretty familiar landmarks.

I contend that whether major or minor, the situations we find ourselves in are always temporary. While some may last longer than others, they will eventually end. Now, some of you just gave your computer (or cell phone) that look as if to say "yeah, but...", but I'm asking you to think about it. If trouble seems to last forever in your life, it's because you failed to really do something about it. And I must remind you that sitting back and hoping things get better is not taking action. Fall to your knees and pray all you want, but faith without works is dead. So get to work.

We must properly analyze our situations so that we don't overreact. Everything isn't as dire as we want it to be. Everything isn't as major as we want it to be. Everything isn't a "Lord, why has Thou forsaken me" situation. Some of it is what we need to learn from. And as we discussed last week, some of it is just a matter of patience. I'm aware that at times, we come across people or circumstances that seem to only exist to complicate our lives. But believe it or not, we can manage those situations too.

We can and should always start by having a healthy appreciation for what we do have in life. For example, in the past, whenever someone would have money troubles, you might hear them say, "Well, at least I have my health". What happen to that sentiment? What happened to that kind of thinking in our lives? Thanking God for what we do have as opposed to crying about what we don't have. If we spent less time looking over our shoulders at who's coming behind us, looking across the street to see what someone else has or just getting into someone else's business, we'd have a better handle on what we have. If we did a better job of managing what God has already given to us, we'd all be better off.

This week, when life pushes you from your center, push back. All is never lost as long as God rules the universe. Remember to be firm on your position as long as you're in the will of God. And in those moments when you find yourself out of your element and off your square, don't despair. As I said, all earthly situations are temporary. We have not reached the point of no return until God says so. If you still feel lost, think of it this way: Whenever I feel as if I'm even a little bit lost, I imagine God providing me with a roadmap back to safety. If I'm ever unsure of where I am, He opens His hands and reveals to me a locator that simply says "You are here".

Resisting the call of misery

Misery loves company. We've all heard that before. All of us know someone that we sometimes hate to see coming because we know that they're bringing all of their problems and issues with them. Those bag ladies and bag men that carry every bit of their troubles with them wherever they go.

No matter the day or hour that you see them, you dare not ask them how they're doing because they're very, very willing to tell you. All the trouble on their job, all the trouble with their health, all the trouble in their love lives, all their financial troubles and so on and so forth (as if you don't have your own problems to deal with). They never tell you that they're fine because in their minds, they never are. But who really is? Who's always 100%? No one, I'm sure. At any given point, we're all dealing with something, whether it be major or minor. It's all in how you deal with it. It's all in whether or not you know what to do when trouble comes your way.

What I've found is that we as a people can be quite miserable at times. When things don't go as we think they should, we take it out on everything and everyone. People that had nothing to do with our current state or mood are forced to feel our wrath on any number of levels. And while it's obviously unfair for any of us to have to deal with another's bad mood when we had nothing to do with it, we allow others to alter our mood and take us in the wrong direction. Because their day has been ruined by whatever it has now become our problem too. Who came up with this philosophy?

This is often very true in the Christian community. Often, when we get ourselves together and pointed in the right direction, others that aren't on that same path will try to hold us back. They try to convince us that we aren't changed by reminding us of who we once were. As we try to move forward, they try to take us backwards by saying "Remember when we used to…" And while you may in fact remember when, that doesn't mean that's who you are now. They try to make us seem as though we're looking down on them by simply lifting ourselves up in Christ. But we must stay on the path that we're on. Once we find ourselves pointed in the right direction, we must remain in the position that God has placed us in.

I'm sure there are some that know me personally that have read these weekly emails that have wondered aloud, "Who does he think he is? I remember him when…" Well, your memory about me may or may not be serving you well. What you know of me may either be fact or it may be fiction. The good thing about it is I'm not worried either way. Because not only do I know who I was or wasn't in my past, I know who I am now and whether the devil likes it or not, I'm comfortable in my beautiful black skin.

For the most part, I never let what another person does or says ruin my day. Sure, we can all get irritated from time to time and it's not always easy, but I'm usually pretty good at letting it go. However, there are times when things may get the best of me. I have my moments of weakness. But this is when we have to be stronger than what's happening to us.

We have to remember to try and put ourselves in a place of peace at all times. If we allow others to control our emotions to the degree where they can ruin our day, we can wind up being just as miserable as they are. The worst thing about it is these people will come into your life, drop their misery on you and move on with their day without giving it another thought. They're comfortable doing so because this is who they are. We're uncomfortable dealing with it because it's not who we are. We have to understand that when people are unhappy they sometimes want everyone else to be unhappy because it seems to make them feel better about their situation. In reality, it doesn't make them feel any better because if their situation doesn't change, they remain in a state of misery.

This week, when they come knocking at your door with their misery, in the words of B.B. King, don't answer the door. Tell 'em to keep it moving. While we should look to help people release their misery and live a better and happier life, we don't exist as banks of misery where they can make a weekly deposit. We don't exist for them to beat on emotionally. We're here to serve a higher purpose. Not only are we here to live a life of joy, we're here to spread joy.

And speaking of that, if you happen to be one of those that insist on weighing the world down with your problems, we need you to make a change. When the world gets you down, we need you to do what we have to do and carry on anyhow sometimes. Because in reality, we have no choice. If you have that much trouble in your life, there is an outlet. Don't take your problems to work with you. Don't take your problem to a place of business and take them out on the people there. Don't take them to social functions where people are trying to enjoy themselves. If you really and truly want to rid yourself of the troubles in your life, there's only once place to take them and that's to God in prayer. Oh, and one last thing. Be sure to leave them there.

Even in the worst of times, the blessings are still there

⁷Ask, and it shall be given you; seek, and ye shall find; knock, and it shall be opened unto you ⁸For every one that asketh receiveth; and he that seeketh findeth; and to him that knocketh it shall be opened ⁹Or what man is there of you, whom if his son ask bread, will he give him a stone? ¹⁰Or if he ask a fish, will he give him a serpent? ¹¹If ye then, being evil, know how to give good gifts unto your children, how much more shall your Father which is in heaven give good things to them that ask Him? — Matthew 7:7-11

In my work, I deal with a lot of relationship issues. What I've found are people that are either unwilling to work hard at a relationship or people that refuse to understand that even a bad relationship has important life lessons that we need to take from the situation. So many times, we assume that some things aren't of God because we happen to be unhappy about where we are. Understand that God doesn't want us to be unhappy, but sometimes He's simply allowing us to have what we've prayed and begged for.

Most times, I believe that God answers our prayers to bless us, but sometimes I believe He answers them to teach us a lesson. Sometimes He answers them so that we can learn to be careful what we pray for. We have to become more aware of what life is about and the ways in which God delivers messages to us. Sometimes they come in the most unflattering ways, but I think they come that way to see if we're really paying attention.

Let's look at work as an example. We're unprofessional in our work at times because we don't like our jobs or we can't see a future in what we're doing. The idea of doing the best that you can because it's just the professional thing to do is sometimes lost on us. Now, you can look at it as if this isn't a job you plan to keep forever, so effort doesn't matter, but I see it differently.

Most of us that tend to be faith based people probably at some point prayed for the job that we currently have. Maybe you were out of work or maybe you were tired of your old job. So now that God has answered your prayers, you have responded by not showing the proper appreciation for what He's given you. You've allowed the job or the fact that you now can't stand what you've asked for to rob you of your professionalism. You've allowed your feelings to compromise your willingness to give your best.

Let me give you one last analogy. Let's say that you have a child that asks you for a particular pair of shoes, and knowing kids these days, they would probably be a pricey pair of shoes. Let's say that instead of those shoes, you buy your child a less pricey, and thus, less popular pair of shoes. Maybe in your mind, you're thinking that you'll see how they treat this pair of shoes before you go head first into a pair of overpriced sneakers.

In response, let's say that this child decides that they will dog the pair of shoes that you've bought them because it isn't what they asked for. They play in them, clean the yard in them, take out the trash in them and so on and so forth. In that child's mind, the thinking may be that these aren't the shoes they wanted, so they don't have to appreciate them as much. But when they get the shoes they really want, they'll treat them as if they were gold. But as the parent looking on from a distance, you're thinking that this kid is crazy. Why would you go out and get them more expensive shoes when it's clear that they can't take care of what you've given them? Are you beginning to understand how God feels when He blesses us?

This week, re-evaluate what God has given you. Take a good look at what's happening in your life and assess it from a different perspective. The things that aren't the best situations may still be a blessing to you. It may not feel like it to you because you're looking at it the wrong way. Even a bad job pays you, puts clothes on your back and food on the table. Go to the unemployment office and see how many are willing to trade places with you. Even a bad relationship can teach you how to be a better partner or teach you that maybe wanting a "thug" or a woman that wears next to nothing regularly isn't really what you wanted. It just seemed like a good idea at the time.

When God gives us what we ask for, it doesn't mean that it's forever. Sometimes we are given things for a season. Sometimes, we are given things so that we can learn something and then move on to the next one. I believe this is why we're stuck in bad relationships for so long. We refuse to learn the lesson that's being taught by the situation, and thus we can't/won't move on.

However, we must always understand that we should give our full appreciation to God for His many, many blessings. If you see that a relationship isn't working out, learn what you're supposed to learn from the situation and then move on. If you're not working the job that God has given you to the best of your ability, you may be holding up your next job. Remember, sometimes God can't replace what we have with something better because we haven't done what we were supposed to do with what we already have.

Week of January 31, 2010

Patience on the road to change

[1]...let us lay aside every weight, and the sin which doth so easily beset us, and let us run with patience the race that is set before us [2]Looking unto Jesus, the author and finisher of our faith, who for the joy that was set before Him endured the cross, despising the shame, and is set down at the right hand of the throne of God – Hebrews 12:1-2

The more things stay the same, the more they need to change. This is something that I've noticed over the past few weeks. While I'm still hearing a lot about people changing for the New Year and changing for other reasons, I still hear and see the same things from all of us. It seems to be a lot of talk with no action behind it. Where are we going with that? All of us have the desire to be better in life than we are today or than we were yesterday. Unless you're the self deprecating kind, all of us wanna be great. But what are you willing to go through to achieve real change? What are you willing to do to be great? Here's my testimony.

I speak a lot about my job in these emails because I feel that that's one of the places that God uses me the most. I feel that I'm being used there to set an example. This is one of the main reasons I stopped complaining about where I worked and the fact that I was unhappy for a time there. I came to realize that God had placed me there for a reason.

There are people there that otherwise may have never met someone like me in their lives. I realized that this was my opportunity to change lives on a smaller scale before I can do it on a larger one. In order to do that, I had to change my life. I had to change my approach. I had to understand what it meant to be "tried by the fire". If I can't do good in situations that aren't the best, then what good can I really do? Isn't that where people need you the most, when things aren't at their best?

I think one of the main reasons that we can't complete our changeover from where we are to something better is because we've convinced ourselves that we can do things instantaneously. To use myself as an example again, I used to say often that as soon as I quit my job, I could really get into my writing and do what I wanna do with all of these thoughts inside my head. But no matter how I tried, I couldn't find another job and my writing kept getting pushed further and further into the background. Soon I realized that the only thing keeping me from writing was me and my unwillingness to use my current situation to my advantage. Two promotions later, I'm 3 published books in, 3 more in the works and I do a weekly email. Needless to say, God's plan worked best.

Real change can't happen overnight. It takes time. I had to understand this just like you do if you're looking for change. By learning to accept my situation, I was able to change. From there, I became a better writer and a better person. And God knows, I was given plenty of material from which to write by staying right where I was. I just had to slow down and take my time.

Look at it this way, God created Heaven and earth in 6 days. Now, I have no doubt that God, in all of His infinite wisdom and strength could've done this in one day. There truly is nothing too hard for God. But, if you will allow me to theorize this thing for a minute, I imagine it took so long because He wanted to take His time. I imagine He wanted to take His time so that He could give every aspect all the love and attention that it deserved. Unlike us, I imagine He didn't wanna do a rush job.

What we must learn to appreciate is the greater plan. We must learn to operate with greater vision. We must learn to be goal oriented in all phases of our lives. If you don't have a vision, a goal and a plan to get there in life, you wind up spinning your wheels. Even those of us in life that reach some level of accomplishment without planning usual self destruct at some point if we don't develop some type of plan to stay successful. Greatness isn't easy. You have to work at it. Even though there were people on that job that wanted me gone just because they didn't like me, God kept me anyway. Some of those same people are long gone now and I'm still there. When The Word says He'll make your enemies your footstool, you better believe it.

This week, do your best to make the best. What that means is realize that the road to success isn't always going to be as smooth as you envisioned it, but that may be the way home. Something else I tell my employees often is if you can't do little things well, then how will anyone know that you can handle big things? If you can't handle tough times, how will you really be able to appreciate the good times? What we're often missing is the right attitude for success. We walk around as though we're owed something. We walk around as though we're entitled to all things great in this life. But anything worth having is worth working for. I thank God for the good times and I thank Him for the bad times. For if I had never existed as a lump of coal, I'd never have this opportunity to shine like a diamond.

Be ye not afraid

[20]And the God of peace shall bruise Satan under your feet shortly... -
Romans 16:20

Are we really aware of how busy Satan is in our day to day lives? Well, he is. Whether you believe it or not, as wonderful as you think you are, there are people out there that not only dislike you and disagree with you on how wonderful you think you are, but if it's within their power, they'll try to bring you down. It's easy to overreact in this situation and act as if the world is crashing down around us, but nothing here is that dire. Until you reach Job status, you shouldn't blow things out of proportion. However, when they come for you, you should be ready to do battle. I don't know about you, but I'm so ready.

The devil has been busy with my family during the first part of this year. He's damaged personal property, caused emotional distress and this past week, he came to me on my job again. Now, I'm not crazy. I didn't suspect that I'd be able to sit here and write email after email each week about the goodness of God and the devil wouldn't come to test me again. But that's the beauty of it all. See, when a person gets strong in any area of their lives, it's because they've found themselves to be weak in that particular area. The problem is we sometimes get lazy when we reach a particular level of strength. We get to a certain point where we can hold our own and then we relax. I don't know about you, but that's not me. I want to go further.

When you reach a certain level of success in your life, the devil is not pleased. However, don't get shortsighted when you hear me speak of success. Don't think of material success. Success comes in many different ways in life. There is financial success, there's career success, there's emotional success, there's success in our relationships and our families, and then there's the most important success, spiritual success.

When we achieve that spiritual success, when we've decided that we will do our best each day to live as God would have us live, this is when we have the devil's attention. This is when he wants to attack you. This is when he wishes to remind you of all of your imperfections. This is when he wants you to believe that you can't do what you've set your mind to do. No matter how successful you've been, this is when he wants you to think that not only are you not as successful as you think you are, but you never will be. But if you're in the right state of mind, this is when you're most prepared. So when he sees that you will not waver and will not be deterred, this is when he's at his most frustrated.

When the devil came to me on my job last week, he sought to tear me down. He sought to make me seem as though I wasn't what I thought I was. He sought to diminish what I had done. But what the devil and his representative didn't quite understand is that when I work out spiritually, I don't do it to get strong, because I'm already strong. When I work out spiritually, I do it to stay strong. I do it because I know that as long as I'm trying to do what God would have me to do, there are gonna be times when the devil is gonna pick a fight. And when that moment comes, I'm never backing down. When that moment comes, I don't know to be afraid of him.

The reality is I'm too old to be running from anything and too brave to be afraid. As I've told him before when he's come to attack me or attack my family, I'm not afraid to fight and if that's what he wants to do, we'll be out in the middle of the street like we don't know each other.

I wrote a piece a couple of years ago called "Fear Is Not An Option". This piece was basically in response to some things that happened on my job. Because man does so many things based on fear and not on what God has told them to do, they will often try and motivate you with the fear that they would feel in their hearts if someone were to try that same tactic on them. However, I always stress to these types of people that they can't place their fears on me. Just because you would be afraid in any given situation doesn't mean that I would be in the same situation. In fact, I'm more likely to be confident because of my makeup. I'm more confident because of how I was raised. I'm more confident because I know that God controls all of this.

This week, stay in shape and stay ready. When things are at their best for us, the devil and his representatives are at their worst. This is not a moment to be afraid. This is not a moment to worry. This is not a moment to act as if all is lost. This is a moment to rely on your training. This is why we worship the way that we do. This is why we study The Word as we do. This is why we serve the God that we serve. Those of us that are doing this right aren't doing it for show. We're not just doing it to get to Heaven. We're doing it so that we can survive down here. We have the tools to defeat Satan and those that represent him. We work out spiritually for a reason. Not so that we can pick a fight, but so that we can always win when they pick one with us.

Ain't no need to worry

²²Cast thy burden upon the Lord, and He shall sustain thee: He shall never suffer the righteous to be moved – Psalm 55:22

As I write these emails each week, one of my goals is to give people a sense of hope. Another is to give people a sense of calm. I want to give people something that my mother gave me long ago. That sense that no matter what the situation, I should not worry. Now, I understand that this isn't easy and no one lives life 100% worry free. But we can get close if we have the right mindset. If we become better at life management, we can become better at living a stress free life. But what I've learned over this last year of writing is no matter how hard you try, you can't teach people not to worry. That's something that they have to develop on their own.

While I do my best not to come off like I'm preaching in these emails, I realize that some people do see this as a source of inspiration. Just from the conversations that I've had with some of you, this message is forwarded so many times that I have no idea how many people read my words on a weekly basis. That's a blessing in itself and I'm truly grateful for all that are a part of my work, but I do wonder how many actually heed what God has given me to say to them. I wonder how many simply enjoy the work like they do church, where they find it gratifying for the moment, say "Amen" when the preacher says something that connects with them, but continues to live their lives the same way.

We need to understand that we do have power here on earth. And while we certainly can't do it all, we must learn to call on God to do our heavy lifting. We must learn to use God to sustain us. We can't seek to wear out God with things that we can control ourselves. This is not to suggest that we have problems that are too small or insignificant for God, it is to suggest that we take care of some of these things ourselves.

While we will all have our burdens in life, they are man made burdens. So if we exercise better judgment at key points in our lives, we can spend more time thanking God for all that He's done for us and less time looking to God to bail us out of another jam.

For example, when we have more bills than we have money, we can call on God in our hour of need. But if you have more bills than money because you poorly managed your money or you decided to go shopping before paying you bills, that's not the time to call on God. That's the time to use the resources that He's already given you (common sense, money management courses, etc.) to make better decisions. Look at it this way, if God has given you a job that can adequately provide for you and your family, do you really need Him to come down and manage that for you?

If you have disobedient or wayward children, it's alright to call on God when you've done all that you can to set them straight. However, if you haven't set the proper example for your children to follow and they're either mimicking your behavior or showing the ramifications of there being no proper guidance in the home, then you shouldn't be looking to just pray this thing away. You should be looking to get yourself together before you get the kids together because doing it the other way won't work. Use the resources given to you here on earth before you just decide to take it to the throne of grace. God has already provided answers to our prayers in many, many situations. He has already alleviated our burdens. Sometimes we're not looking in the right places for the answers, and sometimes we're not looking in the mirror at the right causes for these troubles we're experiencing.

This week, separate your problems like you do your laundry. Light colors on one side, darks on the other and so on. Once you've done that, examine them carefully. If you're looking at a problem that's not serious in nature or one that you could solve yourself if you really put your mind and effort to it, guess what? That means that God has already provided you with the answer. You just have to work for it. So, instead of hitting you knees and saying "Lord, what shall I do", try hitting your knees and saying "Thank you Lord for providing me with that solution". If it's a little too heavy for your arms to carry, do what I do and don't worry. Simply take it to God and leave it with Him. And don't just say "Amen" to what you just read, really trust me on this one. He will sustain you.

Week of May 30, 2010

There is strength when we believe and endure

⁶Rejoiceth not in iniquity, but rejoiceth in truth; ⁷Beareth all things, beliveth all things, hopeth all things, endureth all things – 1 Corinthians 13:6-7

I received a call from a friend last night that was going through some difficulty. As we spoke about what was going on, she seemed to be struggling with some things that were going on in her personal life. She seemed overwhelmed and she said she didn't quite know how to handle all that was on her plate. "I can't continue being Superwoman" she said to me. "What am I supposed to do?" she asked. As I told my Bible class recently, one way or another, I have the answers to your questions. If they're not already in my head, I know where to find them.

Let's start with what we all have on our plates. As a child, I remember my mother fixing my plate and giving me just what she thought I could handle. No more, no less. No matter how much food I thought I could consume – and though I was a small child, my brothers and sisters can attest to the fact that I could consume mass quantities – my mother only gave me what I could and should have had. She knew that a child's eyes can be bigger than their stomach. This is who we are as humans. We always want more than we really need.

Okay, let's deal with the superheroes among us. Now, I've been accused of trying to portray the Man of Steel in my time. But those that really know anything about me know that I'm not so much a Superman guy as much as I am a Batman guy, for reasons that we won't go into here. But, I digress. The reason people saw me that way was because of the fact that I seemed to be able to handle things in ways that others couldn't. I seemed to have a higher tolerance for the trials of life. However, the truth of the matter is I possess nothing that anyone else couldn't if their minds were in the right place. We all either have the knowledge or we have access to it. We just have to put it to use regularly.

What I've chosen to do is practice my faith just as I would anything else that I wanted to perfect. For example, I do this email weekly, but that's not the only thing I write. I do other works in an effort to perfect my craft. My faith deserves the same commitment. Just as it is with everything in life, practice makes perfect. This is definitely true with Christianity. You get better as you go, as long as you stay of the path that The Lord has set for you. If we're willing to put in the necessary time that it takes to learn other things we wanna know, whether they're good for us or not, we have to approach God with the same tenacity. We have to understand that we can't just jump into Christianity. It's a process. It's a journey.

When life gets a little difficult, it's a test of your faith. Are you going to let your circumstances weigh you down or are you going to rise above the situation? That's the question we all have to ask ourselves. We can't say that we have too much on our plate but continue to go to the drama buffet and load up. Doing that, we become full of things that God would rather we didn't have inside of us. We can't sit back and claim that we're not Superwomen or Supermen and continue to try and lift and carry everything on our shoulders. We can't continue trying to save the world when we need help ourselves.

This week, become a practicing Christian. We have to understand that as long as we're here, trials will come. It's a part of life. But we're equipped to handle it all because God's Word is still here as a guide. We must continue to practice our craft because the devil practices his. He's more vigilant when you claim to have confessed Christ as your Savior. It's when you're not practicing your faith regularly that the enemy sneaks in and takes control of your life. Before you know it, you're trying to fight your battles alone and asking God to help you with things while your heart is full of hate and anger. You have to remove such things from your being if God is to help through anything. We should never feel that we're carrying the load ourselves. Remember that you're not in this alone. We struggle when we're alone, but with Jesus at your side, you can't do anything but succeed.

October 8, 2008

"It'll be alright…"

If you've got kids, know kids, have babysat kids or whatever, you've said that before. Bumped heads, scraped knees, parental disappointments and all of that have made us say it a time or two. Sometimes we say it to simply settle the situation down. Sometimes we just want all the noise to stop because kids can get pretty loud when they cry. But barring any major injuries, we're usually saying it because it's the truth. It really will be alright. But what happens when you have to say that to an adult? Believing it will truly be alright takes a great deal of faith.

We as adults can be more dramatic than the children we have to console. We shake our heads at those kids when they cry after a little bump when they fall. A scrape on that knee is like the end of the world. If you didn't know any better, you'd think that the leg would have to be amputated. So quick are we to tell those kids to settle down and stop being so dramatic. It's not that bad. And when we tell them that, we expect them to stop crying immediately. We expect them to trust us when we say "It'll be alright". As it is with so much that adults do, we have a "do as I say and not as I do" feel with the messages we send to our kids.

When faced with adversity in our lives, how many of us truly believe that it will be alright? When I speak of adversity, I'm not just talking about a bad day at work. I'm talking about going to work and finding out that soon, you'll have no work to go to. I'm not talking about having a fight with your mate, I'm talking about finding out that you don't have a mate anymore because your relationship is over. I'm talking about finding out that a loved one isn't sick anymore, they're gone. I'm talking about finding out that your kids aren't what you thought they were. Finding out that your friends aren't who you thought they were. Finding out that there are more that oppose you than you thought there were yesterday. I'm talking about finding out that life's burdens just got a little heavier than they were yesterday. Do you have the same trust that you want that injured child to have? Do you really believe that it will be alright?

Living in the times that we live in, it's so easy to wanna give up. Our faith is tested almost daily. Our mental and physical strength is tested as well. There's war in the world that no one really understands. There's murder in our streets. Our children are in danger. And if you're not in any of the situations that I just mentioned, we all have either had or are currently going through tough financial times. Maybe you've had your heart broken. Maybe your kids won't act right. Maybe you're being tested on your job. All of these things will make you wanna close your eyes forever. But now is not the time. Today is not the day. I submit to you that it will be alright.

Here's what I suggest: When the hour seems its darkest, that's when you must reach deep down inside and pull out the best of you. You mustn't let the weight of the situation pull you under. I want you to trust me in the same way that we want that child to trust us. It will be alright. How do I know? Because it always is. I was once asked by a friend, "Why don't you ever worry?" I told her, "Because I know that things will always work out". How do I know that? Because they always do.

We mustn't confuse things working out with getting what we want. Sometimes we don't get what we want, but things still work out. We're sometimes challenged by life and may have to adapt to some things, but in the end, it all works out. We all swear that we won't survive life's little catastrophes, and yet we wake up each day with an opportunity to conquer life. Why not use that opportunity to change things as opposed to complain about the way things are? If you're reading this then you're living proof that the God you serve has yet to leave your side. No matter how many times you've proclaimed that you're dying, He woke you up again this morning to prove you wrong.

If I ask someone how they're doing and they tell me that they're surviving, I tell them that I know because we have no choice. What else are we gonna do? This past week was very trying for me from a personal standpoint, but through all of the anger, frustration, disrespect and disappointment of the situations I faced, I held on to one thought: It will be alright. While I haven't always kept my end of the bargain, God has never let me down. I have complete faith and confidence that He won't be starting today. No matter what I've gone through in my life, He has brought me out. So when I bump my head, or when life decides to go upside my head, I lay my head on the Father's shoulder. He then tells me, "Don't cry, it'll be alright". And as a child that trusts his parent, I believe Him.

www.ingramcontent.com/pod-product-compliance
Lightning Source LLC
LaVergne TN
LVHW051230080426
835513LV00016B/1505